Praise for Barefoot in Baghdad

"Manal Omar captures the complex reality of living and working in war-torn Iraq, a reality that tells the story of love and hope in the midst of bombs and explosions."

—Zainab Salbi, founder and CEO of Women for Women International, and author (with Laurie Becklund) of the national bestselling book *Between Two Worlds: Escape from Tyranny: Growing Up in the Shadow of Saddam*

"A fascinating, honest, and inspiring portrait of a women's rights activist in Iraq, struggling to help local women while exploring her own identity. Manal Omar is a skilled guide into Iraq, as she understands the region, speaks Arabic, and wears the veil. At turns funny and tragic, she carries a powerful message for women, and delivers it through beautiful storytelling."

—Christina Asquith, author of *Sisters in War: A Story of Love, Family and Survival in the New Iraq*

Barefoot in Baghdad

Barefoot in Baghdad

A Story of Identity—My Own
and What It Means to Be a Woman in Chaos

Published by Sourcebooks, Inc.
P.O. Box 4410, Naperville, Illinois 60567–4410
(630) 961–3900
Fax: (630) 961–2168
www.sourcebooks.com

Library of Congress Cataloging-in-Publication Data

Omar, Manal M.
   Barefoot in Baghdad : a story of identity—my own and what it means to be a woman in chaos / by Manal M. Omar.
      p. cm.
   1. Women—Iraq—Social conditions. 2. Muslim women—Iraq. 3. Muslim women—United States. 4. Iraq—Social conditions. I. Title.
   HQ1735.O43 2010
   305.48'89275670090511—dc22
                              2010010666

Printed and bound in the United States of America.
VP 10 9 8 7 6 5 4 3 2 1

To my parents, Dr. Mohammed and Mrs. Lamah Omar,
and my husband for supporting me
even during times of madness.

CONTENTS

ACKNOWLEDGMENTS

FIRST AND FOREMOST TO MY parents, Dr. Mohammed and Mrs. Lamah Omar, for supporting me always.

A special thanks to my Iraqi staff, past and present. I wish I could name you one by one, but I know how precious your anonymity is. You remain the true silent heroes behind all the great work. Thank you for providing me with the access to know your country intimately, and for always making me feel at home.

Thanks to my editor, Shana Drehs, for her endless patience, and to all the staff at Sourcebooks for their time to make this happen.

A few shout-outs:

To Nadia Roumani for being my rock and mentor and, more specifically, for locking me in her apartment in New York for ten days to write out the first few chapters. And none of that would have even happened without Rhonda Roumani and Annia Ciezadlo convincing me I had a story to tell.

To Corey Saylor, Elizabeth Detwiller, Negina Sawez, and Shirin Sinnar for reading through the entire manuscript and taking the time to give me all the wonderful, and not so wonderful, feedback. Special thanks to Nadine Ajina, Talib Mukhlis, Dr. Anas Ali, and Aisha Ali in the UK for being our family when we were in exile, and for pushing me to finish what I had started.

To Khitam and Saja, for being the powerful Iraqi women that you are and restoring my faith in true sisterhood. To Amena Chenzai, Dalal Al Toukhi, Aunt Vicki Al Toukhi, Tannaz Haddadi, Muna Shami, Nicole Correri, Tooba Mayel, and Tariq Ammous for the constant support.

To Inayet Sahin and Zeena Altalib for being my moral compass.

To Hani: I will always see you as my baby brother and continuously look to you for your wise words.

To the amazing women who constantly remind me of our inner strength. I am blessed to have had your support on Iraq: Lady Anne Greenstock, Edit Schleffer, Khanim Latif, Laila Noureldin, Lucie Aslou, Magda El Sanousi, Oroub Al Abed, and Zainab Salbi.

To the future: my nieces and nephews Noor, Jude, Mohammed, and Abdul Malik Omar; Raya, Marya, and Petra Mufti; Adam and Zaid Omar; Fatima, Ali, and Hamza Al Dubaisi. You are the source of all my optimism.

And most importantly, thanks to my husband. I would not have remembered half the stories or the details without you. Thanks for being my solid foundation, and keeping me grounded always.

Author's Note

Names, geographic locations, and identifying characteristics have been changed to protect those whose stories are shared. This is my personal journey; the views expressed are my own and do not represent the policy of Women for Women International.

Barefoot in Baghdad takes its title from a popular Iraqi-Turkmen proverb that says, "Walk barefoot and the thorns will hurt you." It is often used as a warning to those who challenge societal norms.

INTRODUCTION

Throughout my childhood I struggled to answer the simplest of questions: where are you from? I was born in Saudi Arabia to Palestinian parents who moved to Lubbock, Texas, when I was six months old. During my childhood, my parents would uproot me every few years, from Texas to South Carolina to Virginia. Living in the American South, I was far from the image of a Southern belle, and yet the summers I spent in the Middle East only emphasized my American identity and made it clear to me that I would also never exactly be an Arab poster child.

By the time I was in high school, I had learned to embrace and love all parts of my joint identity with the fervor only a teenager could feel. I was an Arab and an American. I was a Palestinian and a Southerner. I was a Muslim and a woman. As I grew, I accepted that the emphasis on each facet of my identity would shift with the

phases of the moon. Growing up in a world struggling to understand multiculturalism, I saw this ability to move among my many
identities as my own secret superpower.

Propelled by the conviction that my identities provided me
with a competitive advantage, I embarked on a career in international development. My mother argued that somewhere along
the way I became delusional, perhaps because my desire to make
a difference in the world led me to a career in humanitarian aid in
conflict zones.

With my secret superpower tucked away, I was among the first
international aid workers to arrive in Baghdad in 2003. I would also
be among the last to leave. The two intervening years inside Iraq
would transform my life forever.

Many writers have attempted to capture in words what
happened in Iraq during the watershed years of 2003 through early
2005. Some authors have written about the political maneuvering
behind the walls of the Green Zone or the military strategy as
seen by journalists embedded in the armed forces. But until now,
none of them have written from the viewpoint of an international
aid worker who had access to both everyday Iraqi citizens and the
people in power on the U.S. and Iraqi sides.

In Iraq, I was finally able to put my superpower to full use.
A wave of my American passport at the checkpoint of the fortified Green Zone allowed me access to the representatives of the
U.S.-led coalition. My adherence to Muslim dress and my fluent
Arabic made it possible for me to live in an Iraqi neighborhood
with no armed security. This unique access allowed me to see an
Iraq that was accessible to few others. With each passing season,
the country would shed its skin from the past and emerge as a
completely new place. Who was better positioned to adapt within a
country experiencing a period of tumultuous change than someone
who had been raised with an ever-shifting identity? In Iraq, I found

a place with as many complicated contradictions as I had in myself. Here, though, my internal complexity was manifested in an entire society. My international colleagues were struggling to force Iraqi culture into convenient boxes, but I simply accepted its unique, fluctuating shape. International journalists marveled over the fact that women who were covered head to toe walked side by side with women with orange-colored hair and wearing tight jeans, but I simply shrugged. It was natural to me. The mosaic of identities inside Iraq was not hypocritical or schizophrenic; it was what made the country powerful.

Nevertheless, that mosaic was shattered by the eruption of violence that followed on the heels of the U.S. invasion. From weapons of mass destruction to suicide bombings, the lives of everyday Iraqis became inextricably linked to violence. The hopes and dreams that Iraqis once dared to share evaporated in the smoke of car bombs. The diverse peoples who populated Iraq—Arabs, Kurds, Assyrians, Muslims, Christians, Sabaeans—had once sipped tea at their doorsteps, but now they had disappeared from the streets. Women hid behind closed doors. The only images from within Iraq were of death and destruction. The only feelings people described were betrayal and despair. Overnight, that brilliant diversity—Iraq's own secret superpower—was forgotten, buried under the rubble left by bombs.

* * *

My story is not one of statistics and death tolls or descriptions gleaned from short visits to the Green Zone. Instead, my story outlines the journey of a nation determined to rise from the ashes of war and sanctions and to re-create itself in the face of overwhelming obstacles. But this is also my own story of struggling to understand my identity against the backdrop of a country in turmoil. What I experienced internally reflected what the country as a whole was enduring. As a woman, I could not bear to see the erosion of the simple freedoms Iraqi women had gained decades earlier. Gone were the days when Iraqi woman could walk in the streets unaccompanied or choose what they would wear.

As a non-Iraqi Arab, I felt apologetic toward the Iraqis, who were baffled as to why Arabs from other countries were coming to Iraq to act as suicide bombers in crowded markets and on buses. And I was angry to witness the most powerful nation in the region being torn apart.

As an American, I was speechless. I could neither attack nor defend my country, although I found myself desperately wanting to do both. My parents had realized the American dream, and I refused to believe that freedom and democracy were empty promises. But I could not exonerate the United States for its role in allowing Iraq to devolve into violence. The military's most basic mistakes—not securing the borders, dissolving the Iraqi military, and fast-forwarding the nation-building process—had catapulted the country into chaos.

In addition to coming to terms with the war and the violence that unfolded before me, I also had to deal with the implications of my growing personal attachments. My Iraqi staff, my neighbors, and local women's organizations were taking great risks of being labeled traitors or Western puppets just by being associated with me. And yet I found myself developing my own family circle inside the country. The Iraqi women I worked with side by side became my sisters, and the men who risked their lives for my security became my brothers. I desperately wanted to prove my worth by making the lives of the Iraqis a little better, if not those who lived in the communities where I worked, then at least those closest to me. I avoided the thought that one day I would have to leave the country. And I refused to admit that my growing feelings of trust and admiration for one of my male colleagues could actually be love. Eventually, I would be both punished and rewarded for allowing the lines between work and my personal life to blur. Personal tragedy began to strike everyone I knew, one family at a time. People with whom I was close began to disappear without a trace.

Barefoot in Baghdad is not a story of the war in Iraq. It is the story of the women in Iraq who are standing at the crossroads every dawn. It is the story of my time working with Iraqis as they struggled to create a new nation and a new identity. It is informed by my years of living and working within communities throughout the country. It recounts my own experiences and the stories of the men and women I encountered, each of them players in one of the most complicated political struggles of our era. It is also a memoir of the discovery of my many identities and the strengths and weaknesses inherent within them. Finally, it is a story of finding love in the most unlikely place. As my life became intertwined with the lives of the Iraqis around me, I lost sight of where my horizons ended and theirs began. Their expectations became my expectations; their disappointments, dreams, pains, and losses became my own.

Chapter
One

THE OPENING

S HE WAS HIDING. THEN AGAIN, everyone seemed to be hiding. It was October 2003, eight months into the disastrous U.S.-led invasion of Iraq.

But she was practically a child. And her enemy proved to be more insidious—and heartbreaking—than the ones we read about and saw on television.

Getting to her was my first hurdle. That meant having to clear a checkpoint, one of thousands erected across Baghdad. These makeshift sites were thrown together like a neighborhood potluck, except instead of franks and beans, it was a somber medley of military sandbags, Iraqi and American police, and machine guns.

One of the police officers—an older one, with a thick trademark Iraqi moustache—stood to give me the third degree. Who was I? What did I want? The veil wrapped around my head did nothing to assuage his concerns. After all, Baghdad was teeming with American journalists and aid workers who wore the veil out of respect for local customs. He had no reason to believe that I was Muslim just because I said so.

Having to prove myself was nothing new to me. I am a Muslim American, an oxymoron according to some. Back home, I'd grown accustomed to pledging my allegiance louder and more often than my peers. But affirming my allegiance to Islam? This was a first.

The police officer leaned forward and demanded that I recite the first chapter of the Koran, something Muslims recited five times a day during prayer. It was like asking a Christian to say the Lord's Prayer.

Yusuf, one of my colleagues, lit a cigarette and stared, curious if I would pass muster.

The semicircle of gun-toting men, combined with my light-headedness from abstaining from food and drink all day—this incident occurred during the holy month of Ramadan—was making it difficult to recall the seven verses. But I closed my eyes, and within seconds the words came spilling out.

My questioner—to borrow a phrase—was shocked and awed. He returned my passport and waved Yusuf and me through. But not before raising one salt-and-pepper eyebrow: "*Ikhtee, al bint moo raaha* (My sister, the girl is shady)." It was the worst thing a man could say about a woman, that she lacked honor. He, of course, was referring to the girl inside. But his words also served as a warning to me. He was suggesting that I should think twice before cavorting with such people.

I grabbed my passport. The chapter he'd chosen to test my identity—and my faith—was called *Al Fatiha* (the Opening). Indeed, it had served as my opening to gain access to the girl.

Once inside the police building, an Iraqi police officer and a U.S. Military Policeman (MP for short) practically tackled me in an effort to argue their case. Their words were a cacophony of conflicting reports. The Iraqi officer insisted that U.S. soldiers had no legal right to hold the girl in custody. He argued that she was underage, and should her husband or father appear, her male guardians could accuse the Iraqi government of kidnapping her. The American MP laughed at the mention of the government and stated that the United States was in power now. He believed the girl's allegation that she'd be killed the moment she was released from the police station.

Both men were right. She would be killed if she were released. But the police had no authority, under Iraqi law, to hold her.

Luckily for me, I didn't have to make any decisions. I wasn't there to judge or referee. My sole purpose was to ensure that the girl was safe, clothed, fed, and healthy.

"I'm only here to speak with the girl. May I please see her?"

The Iraqi policeman stepped forward and pointed to a room behind him. I nodded to Yusuf, indicating that he should stay and try to get the Iraqi policemen's version of the story.

I opened the door to a small room furnished with the bare essentials: stove, teapot, refrigerator, and square folding table. The girl sat in the opposite corner, her knees pulled into her chest, her chin resting on top. She rocked back and forth, barely noticing that I'd entered. I'm not sure what I'd expected, but the sight of her shocked me. Her skin practically hung from her bones, and the long, thick black hair stretching down her back emphasized her frailty. She was a child trapped in an old woman's body.

I quietly walked toward her and sat next to her. I wasn't sure how to begin, so I said hello and introduced myself.

She continued to rock, saying nothing.

The two of us sat together in silence for what felt like hours, but probably only a few minutes passed. She finally spoke and told me that her name was Kalthoum. Then she offered me tea.

When she stood, I realized why the Iraqi policeman said that he couldn't protect her, not even against his own officers. The way she was dressed—in tight Capri jeans and a low-cut tank top—would have offended even the most liberal Iraqi men.

The elite women in Iraq refrained from donning the veil. The liberal ones wore jeans or short skirts. Kalthoum reached far beyond these bounds.

She needed new clothes. That was essential. I left her briefly to instruct Yusuf to go buy some.

When I returned, Kalthoum had poured two cups of tea. "How can you help me?" she asked, smiling. I was impressed that she could be so pragmatic at age sixteen.

She was less impressed with my response.

"I'm not sure I can. But before I can make that determination, I need to know exactly who you are and what's happened to you."

"I am sure they told you I am a prostitute," she said sheepishly. "Those hypocrites out there. One of them used to be my client. That is why they are so eager to get me out."

The man, one of the police officers, had used her for sex, and now he wanted her released and left for dead. This was not, as one might expect in the United States, because he was ashamed of having patronized a prostitute. To the contrary, in Iraq it was not uncommon for men to engage in such behavior. They did so openly and without remorse. But the judgment of a prostitute? Death. So the very man who had slept with Kalthoum wanted her to die because of it.

"Kalthoum," I said, suddenly curious if that was her real name, "I'm not going to pretend to know what you're going through. But I need you to tell me exactly what happened. Who were the men who were shooting at you? Also, do you have a place you can go, other than here?"

She shook her head as her eyes filled with tears. The men who'd chased her were her husband and brother-in-law. Three years ago her family had forced her to marry her cousin. She was thirteen at the time. She took a photo from her wallet and showed me a picture of her in a wedding gown next to a man old enough to be her father. On her wedding night, she did not want to have sex. So her new husband had beaten and raped her. This, according to Kalthoum, became their normal form of intimacy. He pulled her out of school and locked her in his house. She had considered killing herself.

Then the Americans invaded Iraq. That same week, Kalthoum ran away. An older woman found her on the streets and offered her food and shelter. The woman had nursed her back to health and gave her pills to ease her pain. Soon Kalthoum became addicted. At the time, she didn't realize that the woman was the head of a prostitution ring.

I'd heard many similar stories. But hearing them firsthand from Kalthoum, a child, made me sick.

"I meant every word I said. I want to make sure you have food, shelter, and good health care. And if we can get you out of this place, and you decide to continue with the older woman, I want you to protect yourself from disease and unwanted pregnancies."

"You are too late for that," she said in a barely audible whisper as tears filled her eyes. She put her hand on her stomach to indicate that she was already pregnant.

I closed my eyes. The sun had now begun its descent. The city curfew would begin in a few hours. I, too, had to get out of this place.

I hugged Kalthoum and explained that I would return first thing the next morning. I asked if she would do me a favor and change into the clothes I had sent Yusuf to buy for her. She was ecstatic at the prospect of new clothes, if for no other reason than to get the Iraqi police to stop treating her like trash.

I hoped Yusuf had returned with the goods. When I went to

check, the American MP stood in my way. "Sorry ma'am, you can't go anywhere."

"Excuse me?" I asked confrontationally.

He pointed toward the window behind me. I turned and looked outside. Dozens of men now swarmed the checkpoint. The MPs and most of the Iraqi police were blocking them, refusing them entry.

"The girl's entire family is outside. Her husband, her brothers, and her father are all demanding that we hand her over. We're not sure what we'll do. But the Iraqi police tell me, if you go out, you'll be the new target of their rage. Ma'am, you're an American, and you're my responsibility now."

I glanced outside. Kalthoum's family looked like they were out for blood. The MP was right. If they saw me, it would incite them. If they broke through and got to Kalthoum, there was no doubt that they'd kill her. Considering that Iraqi law protects the father and husband in such situations, they had nothing to lose. I had to hide, to get out of their sight.

We were all stuck.

* * *

The decision to go to Iraq was not mine alone. It was a family affair. When I first sat with my parents to tell them that I wanted to accept a yearlong job in Baghdad, they had stared at me in disbelief.

My father pointed out that I had a great job in Washington DC. It was a job, according to my mother, that anyone would kill for.

It was true. I had enjoyed working at the World Bank for three years, but I was ready to move on. As a former student of international relations, my goal had always been to directly help people in developing countries. Instead, I was sitting comfortably in a high-rise glass office building in the world's most developed nation. I wanted to do more.

"Is this your way of telling us you were fired?" my mother

asked, refusing to believe any sane daughter of hers would leave a prestigious multinational institution for a small unknown nongovernmental organization (NGO) job with half the paycheck.

I launched into an explanation one more time. I desperately needed my parents to try to understand that this was an opportunity of a lifetime. I had been offered the position of country director with Women for Women International, a group that helped female survivors of war to rebuild their lives.

Iraq had already played a monumental role in my own life. I started my career, back in 1997, in Baghdad. I was a reports officer with the United Nations' Oil-for-Food Program. Fear of Saddam Hussein led to explicit orders that we were not to mix with any locals. This was more for their safety than ours. I'd always promised myself that I would return to Baghdad under different circumstances.

I explained to my parents that this was my chance to live out my dream of helping communities from the bottom up.

My father sat silently. Being a daddy's girl meant never being denied anything. I said a silent prayer that Dad wouldn't start saying no now.

"I get it," he said. "I see why you would want to leave the bank. But I don't think you should start with Iraq or any other dangerous place. We are still not over the scare you caused in Afghanistan last month. And I don't think you should go with a small organization. This type of work needs a large organization that can support its staff in the field." His tone was firm, indicating that this was his final answer and there was no room for negotiation.

Bringing up Afghanistan felt like a low blow. I had been in Kabul at the head of a delegation of American women for International Women's Day when the United States invaded Iraq. The U.S. Embassy had ordered all Americans to go into "hibernation," the official lingo for laying low. Translation: I hunkered down inside the Mustafa Hotel near Chicken Street, the most popular expatriate area in Kabul, and watched *Sex and the City* DVDs. Our biggest scare was the television conking out.

I ignored my father's statement and continued to press my case, this time appealing on a more personal level. He'd heard me speak in the past about Baghdad's beauty. I reiterated how I'd fallen in love with the city: the leisurely boat rides down the Tigris River, the bookstores lining Mutanabi Street, the strong Arabic coffee.

It wasn't working.

"If you must help someone, help your own relatives in Palestine," my mother shot back bitterly. "I just don't understand. Your boss used to love you. Why would he fire you?"

I sighed. My mother was a lost cause. My father seemed slightly more persuadable. Then he shook his head. The answer was no. This didn't bode well. He was a man of few words, and I knew they were final when he uttered them. He took his time to make a decision, but once he had decided, it was almost impossible to overturn his verdict. Almost. After all, I was my father's daughter, and I had inherited the same determination.

Next up were my three brothers and my sister, Rula. Normally Rula was a staunch ally, but she couldn't be depended upon in this go-around. She told me that she was unwilling to lose her only sister to a war with which we all disagreed.

Meanwhile, I continued meeting with the management of Women for Women. The main logistics officer was leaving for Iraq in the first week of June to begin preparing the groundwork for an office. I was to follow him a month later.

Thus began a series of family meetings in my brother's basement in northern Virginia. I respected my parents too much; I couldn't go without their approval. Meeting after meeting I presented my case, and each time I was shot down. It was the first time the Omars were united against something—me. Nothing could convince my family that my need to go to Iraq was logical. I shifted tactics and tried to get them to see that I had something to offer. My experience and studies, coupled with my background as an Arab Muslim, were needed in the country.

"Nobody is in Iraq except CIA agents and preachers," my father insisted.

"Maybe so, but that just makes it more important for me to be there!" I shot back.

By the third meeting, I was beginning to get through. Or perhaps I'd just worn them down. Regardless, their responses became less hostile and more geared toward what I would be doing when I was in Iraq. Where would I live? What did the program have to offer?

I began to explain the program of Women for Women International to my father. It began with a sponsorship program, where every enrolled woman was matched with a sister from a developed country, mostly from the United States. The program gave Iraqi women cash to help with the immediate effects of the war, such as food, water, medicine, and other necessities. They also received emotional support in the form of letters.

Women for Women International focused on the most vulnerable women. This usually meant those who were the primary breadwinners in their house: widows, divorcees, or unmarried women living with elderly parents. In addition to the economic challenges, there was a social stigma attached to these women. This meant that their finding work was even more difficult.

The program I would be helping to establish would support women on two levels. First, the program addressed the pragmatic challenges of securing food, water, and shelter. Our main objective was to train the participants in a job skill that would enable them to earn an income. Second, the program hosted bimonthly sessions in which women would discuss ways to improve their lives.

A large portion centered on protecting their rights. At the same time, we would organize awareness workshops centered on health care, family planning, and access to education. The experience of Women for Women International demonstrated that women could only be prepared for the second level of training when their basic needs had been addressed.

I explained to my family that Zainab Salbi had founded the organization. As an Iraqi American born and reared in Iraq, she was herself a war survivor. I was inspired by her because she refused to be a victim and channeled her experience into helping women worldwide. Since its formation in 1993, Women for Women International positively affected more than five hundred thousand family and community members in seven countries.

And now Zainab was offering me an opportunity to join them.

"So how much money are we talking about?" Rula asked.

"Around fifteen dollars," I answered.

"*Jad?* (Seriously?)" my father interrupted. "Is this program serious? You plan to give Iraqi women fifteen dollars? We are talking about Iraq: one of the richest Arab countries, a country that had one of the best education and health infrastructures in the world. You want to go to this rich country, and you think you can help them by giving them peanuts. Not only will it be useless, it will be offensive!"

It was the first time I had seen my father so upset that he stood up and walked out on me. My brothers scowled at me and followed. I didn't have a chance to explain that, like the United States, there were pockets of poverty in Iraq. Not everyone was rich. And in the impoverished areas, fifteen dollars was the difference between starving and feeding your family.

I cried, not because of what my father said, but the way in which he said it. For the first time, my father's face was filled with disappointment when he looked at me. The whole time I had been fighting to go to Iraq, I had believed the only obstacle was my personal security. I began to realize that I was in the midst of an ideological battle as well. For my Palestinian family, the Iraq War hit a raw nerve. My parents saw the war as a reminder of what had happened to the Palestinians in 1948. It was another humiliation of the Arab world at the hands of the West. And as far as they could tell, I wanted to be a part of it—and I was on the wrong side.

The disappointment my parents continued to express pained me deeply. My mother cried every night and took every opportunity to wail her woes at community gatherings. At several family events my mother would complain about how her daughter was punishing her.

"If I only knew what my crime was, I would try to make amends," she said. "But I did all I could to give her a better life. I just do not understand it. We sacrifice everything to take our children out of a war zone, and this one keeps running back in!"

My father's suffering was less open. He would pull me aside and talk to me; he would say he was trying to talk some sense into me. In one of our conversations, he lectured me about the wiles of the CIA, who he said had a history of recruiting idealists like me. At one point he actually believed I would be working secretly for American intelligence.

"You may think you are helping, but you are not," he warned me. "The best way to help our people is by getting the best degrees and being the best at what we do. That way we earn respect that nobody can deny. Your success here is more valuable than anything you can do back there."

A part of me wanted to pull back and be a good Arab Muslim daughter, but something inside me refused. I had an opportunity to make a difference. I was frustrated with watching people sit on the sidelines and complain about George Bush's war and the destruction of Iraq. I had seen the same passivity during the UN-imposed sanctions on Iraq after the 1991 Gulf War. By 2003 the sanctions had crippled the Iraqi economy and devastated the infrastructure. UN agencies had reported the deaths of approximately half a million children as a result of the sanctions. There was a ton of rhetoric about crimes against humanity, but little action was ever taken. Now—after the U.S.-led invasion—Iraqi civilians were left once again to suffer. Malnutrition, illness and disease, inadequate housing. The people lacked the basic necessities of life.

I wanted to stop talking and start doing.

We hit a crossroads as a family. Nobody was willing to back down. My father would not agree, and I would not stop trying. It was getting closer to the end of June, and I was scheduled to leave in two weeks. My brothers and sister were angry with me for what I was doing to our parents. But I couldn't let that stop me from lobbying to make my case.

In the end, I would not go if my father did not give me his blessing. This was a line that would never be crossed. I knew it, and my father knew it. Yet my father never used his veto power casually. It pained him to stand in my way. I was resolved to listen to his final word, but I also owed it to myself to try everything I could to convince him up to the last minute.

Apparently my parents had the same strategy. Wherever I went, family friends pulled me aside and lectured me. "Do you know what you are doing to your mother?" they would ask. I would nod, listen to the lecture, and walk away more determined than ever.

I had grown to expect such encounters. What I hadn't expected was that my close friends began to confront me as well. Most of my friends worked in the same field of international development. Many were avid human rights activists. I had expected their unconditional support. Instead, I received more disappointment and criticism. They argued that no matter how I spun it, my decision portrayed support for the Bush administration. Any success in Iraq equaled a Bush success.

In short, I was seen as a sell out from every angle.

I had reached a breaking point. I needed to get away and think things through. Ever since I was in high school, I had found peace at the Shenandoah River in West Virginia. I went online and booked a room at a small bed-and-breakfast in West Virginia. It was only a one-hour drive from my apartment in DC. I left a phone message at home that I was spending the night out. It was time for some hard-core soul-searching.

Was all this worth the pain I was causing my parents? Was I really selling out and too dense to see it? Was I really trying to make a difference or was this some narcissistic way of seeking attention?

I spent all night praying *Istikhara*, a special prayer for Muslims to help them with difficult decisions. The next morning I awoke with more clarity on the situation than I had had in weeks. This was something I had to do. I had just turned twenty-eight, and if I didn't seize control of my life now, I never would.

I made a final plea to my father. Armed with modern technology I plotted the best way to make my case. Email. I sent a long email to my father, outlining my arguments once more. The final paragraph read:

Dad, it goes without saying that ur word will always be the final word. I know none of the above can convince u, but at the end of the day I am asking u to have faith in me and trust me. I need to do this. I believe I can help. And I could never do this without your blessing.

After I sent the email, I drove back to Virginia. When I arrived home, I found my father's brief reply in my in-box:

I do not know what satanic force is dragging you to Iraq, but I do know I cannot stop you. Go and may God bless you.

It wasn't exactly the father-daughter correspondence I had imagined, but it would have to do. My mother was insistent that I was playing with fire, but she knew that once my father had agreed, there was little more to be said. Indeed, all things immediately fell into place.

On July 4, 2003, I left from Washington Dulles International Airport for Amman, Jordan. The poignancy of traveling on Independence Day was not lost on me as I reflected on countless debates I'd had over Iraq's status between liberation and occupation. Despite our disagreements, all my friends and family came to the airport to bid me farewell. I felt grateful for those in my life. As much as they opposed my decision, they gave me the freedom to make it. When the time came, they were by my side to wish me good luck.

Even my mom came to the airport. Reluctantly, she hugged me and, through her tears, warned me that I may have tricked my dad, but she was still not happy with my decision. For that, she promised me, if I died, the family would hold no funeral services.

In return, I promised to haunt her.

Chapter
Two

ROAD TRIP

I WAS SCARED. I KNEW I had no real reason to be, but I couldn't
help it. It was 3:30 a.m., and I was standing outside a hotel
parking lot in Jordan and waiting for my ride to Baghdad. Our plan
was to drive to the Jordan-Iraq border. We would wait until sunrise
to cross into Iraq, and then we would speed across the country like
the devil was chasing us.

I was actually going to do this. I couldn't quite believe it.

Less than twenty-four hours ago I had boarded my flight at
Washington Dulles, filled with anticipation. The moment I had
spent three months fighting for had arrived. But somewhere along
the line, a feeling of dread overtook me. Instead of shouting for
joy, I wanted to turn and run.

Why hadn't I flown to Baghdad? Well, there were no official
flights. Traveling by road was the only option. But no one had

secured the roads between the border and Iraq's capital. Coffee shops in Amman were filled with stories of travelers who had never made it to their destinations. Highway robberies, once punishable by death under the Saddam regime, were common. What's more, the primary bridges into the city had been bombed, making travelers depend on alternative routes. Although the Saddam regime had been toppled from formal power, the Baathists now controlled the peripheries around Baghdad. Everyone knew they were in charge of all civilian traffic into the country.

The most dangerous travel in Iraq was the journey I was about to embark on.

To make matters worse, I was traveling into Iraq with Zainab Salbi, an icon of women coping with war and its aftermath. She had founded Women for Women International in 1993 in Bosnia and Herzegovina, and since then the organization has opened offices in such war-torn areas as the Congo, Nigeria, and Afghanistan. Zainab herself was honored in 1995 by President Bill Clinton for her work in Bosnia and Herzegovina, and she was named *Time* magazine's Innovator of the Month and received *Forbes* magazine's 2005 Trailblazer Award. She is one of the few nongovernmental organization leaders to be featured on *The Oprah Winfrey Show*, and she has been Oprah's guest five times.

Being around Zainab was intimidating for me. I was constantly filled with self-doubt. I thought, *I've made a mistake. Look at this woman! She is so calm and in control. This is a woman who knows what she is doing. This is a woman who goes inside a war-torn country to help other women. I'm not this woman!*

While I stood and worried in front of the hotel, Zainab bid her younger brother an elaborate farewell. She hugged him, pinched his cheeks, and hugged him again. I could not shake off the feeling that I did not belong on this journey. It didn't help matters that the airline had lost my luggage. I clung to my only possession:

a messenger bag. The contents of the bag were all I had now: my passport, my iPod, a miniature first aid kit, a book, lip balm, antiseptic wipes, and a small copy of the Koran. The realization made me feel even more pathetic.

We did receive some good news. A few other SUVs had radioed in to say they would meet us at the border, so we would now be traveling in a convoy of four Jordanian GMCs instead of a single vehicle. Our driver still looked nervous, but as we pulled out of the parking lot, Zainab began to chat with him. Where was he from? How long had he driven the Amman-Baghdad route? Where did he think Saddam was hiding? I tried to enter into my own trance and zone them out. Her voice was far too cheerful for 4 a.m.!

Zainab began to rummage through the cooler her brother had brought her. "Anyone want falafel?" she asked as she unwrapped a sandwich.

The driver chuckled. I tried to play it cool and laugh quietly as well, but it came out more as a snort. How could she eat at a time like this? I wanted to remind her where we were going. Baghdad. Into a country that was in the middle of war—no matter what President Bush said.

She pulled out an inflatable U-shaped pillow and a matching eye mask, which she placed over her short cropped hair that made her look like her brother's identical twin.

"I'm going to take a nap," she announced to the driver. "If we run into any highway bandits or a roaming al Qaeda cell, make sure to wake me up. I don't want to miss the excitement." With that, she disappeared into the backseat.

Now, there was a true adrenaline junkie. Any excitement I had initially felt about going to Baghdad was long gone.

Playing the role of advocate for the last few months had forced me into a position of offense, and I had not even had a moment to entertain the many doubts and fears that I harbored inside. This eighteen-hour ride gave me plenty of time to catch up.

* * *

It wasn't until I reached Baghdad that I began to understand the full extent of the risk I was taking by launching an office dedicated to marginalized women in Iraq. Despite the fact that the ride into Baghdad was uneventful, worst-case scenarios of life in the city were storming through my mind.

The insurgency would team up with al Qaeda and make Iraq a living hell.

I would be kidnapped.

I would be arrested by U.S. troops because of a mistaken identity.

I would be caught in a crossfire between American troops and the Baathists.

Over my corpse a debate would rage about what to place on the tag identifying me: traitor or terrorist?

My imagination ran wilder with each passing hour. Despite Zainab's reassurance (she had been in these kinds of situations before, and she knew what the odds were like), I could not let my guard down. I became convinced that Iraq was destined to be another Vietnam, and I was struggling with the idea that in a few days Zainab would be returning to Washington DC—and I would be left behind.

I tried to share my thoughts indirectly with Zainab. Each time, she responded with an unmistakable look of sternness in her dark brown eyes. Without saying a word, the look warned me that if I had cold feet, I had better get over it. Pronto! That was the only choice. She had taken a leap of faith in hiring a twentysomething as the country director, and my calling it quits at the eleventh hour would embarrass us both. Yet there was also a kindness in her look. A sort of encouragement touched her smile, and it made me ashamed to admit my doubt. Great. I had managed to add a new item to my list of fears: disappointing Zainab.

I desperately tried to put aside my worries and concerns so I could simply absorb the city as it was.

* * *

Zainab was ecstatic to be in her home country and with her family. From the moment we arrived, we stayed with her maternal uncle. His house was tucked into the corner of the Al Khadamiyah district, where large concrete walls separated the houses from one another. Inside the cold walls, the warmth of her extended family was waiting for us.

Zainab bounced out of the car and disappeared through the gate. A young man came out of the guardhouse and began unloading our luggage. Well, Zainab's luggage. I followed her through the gate.

The minute I passed through the gate I was greeted by two dogs. They ran circles around my ankles and took turns trying to jump onto my thighs. Since childhood I had been a fan of dogs, so I crouched down to their eye level, patting one on his stomach with the palm of my hand while the other ran around me. I was so pleased at seeing my new canine friends that I didn't notice an older man standing nearby and watching me.

"Definitely *Americeeyah*," he said as he offered his right hand in greeting.

Americeeyah—the term Arabs use to refer to Americans. Most Arabs and Muslims have a strong dislike for dogs, since canines are considered to be ritually impure by the majority of both the Sunni and Shia branches of Islam. The only exception is within the Maliki school of Islamic thought, of which I was an adherent.

I stood up. I was embarrassed to offer my hand to him after the dogs had licked it.

"A bit of a mutt myself," I smiled back and offered my hand anyway. I figured it would be worse to leave his hand hanging.

The man's handshake was firm, and the big smile he offered while balancing a cigar at the tip of his mouth was reflected in his deep gray blue eyes. He was about five feet eight, with a trademark large Iraqi belly that made him look like he was nine months' pregnant with twins, and he radiated confidence and warmth. Whoever he was, I knew I liked him. Something about him automatically put me at ease.

Zainab came rushing out of the house and flung herself into his arms. "This is Uncle Fahad, my favorite person in the world," she said.

His smile stretched toward both ears. She was clearly his favorite niece.

Zainab quickly introduced me, and we turned toward the house. It was a large modern home with a small pool in front. It was what lay behind the house that took my breath away. The house was built on the banks of the Tigris River, which runs through the city of Baghdad. A shiver ran up my spine as I looked out on the historic waterway that is mentioned in the Bible twice and was the lifeline of the ancient Sumerians.

I was reminded of how my love affair with Baghdad had begun, back in 1997, when I was here with the UN. Once I realized that every street corner possessed a piece of culture, art, or history, with Nahrain—the two rivers of the Tigris and the Euphrates—as the inspiration, I fell in love. I was ecstatic to be back.

By the side of the pool was a small garden with patio chairs. Three young boys were running around the chairs, playing an imaginary game of war and hiding behind imaginary walls while shooting at each other with plastic guns. Zainab shook her head and turned to her uncle.

"This is the problem with Iraq. From a young age, we give our boys guns and raise them on violence."

Uncle Fahad smiled. "It's *broblem* with all world, my dear."

Overall Fahad's English was very good, with the obvious exception of the constant substitution of *b*'s for all *p*'s. There is no equivalent letter *p* in the Arabic alphabet, and so many Arabs replace it with a *b*. Growing up, my siblings and I would roll with laughter whenever one of our parents would order a *Bebsi* instead of a Pepsi. We teased our parents mercilessly to the point that they would overemphasize their *p*'s when they were in public. Sometimes they were so flustered that they compensated for all the years of mispronouncing *p*'s by replacing all their *b*'s. So *bikini* turned into *pikini*, and *bike* into *pike*. The end result was that I was fluent in an emerging pigeon English language and could easily understand Uncle Fahad.

We left the boys. Uncle Fahad placed his hand in mine and led me into the living room. As we relaxed on the couch, he explained what he saw as the state of the country.

"Iraq is very safe," he said. "No listen to Arab satellite channels. Every Iraqi *habby* we finish with horrible *dick-ta-toor* Saddam. Our country has never had *obbortunity* to see its *botential*. Now it has. And that is scary for many our neighbors."

I nodded as he spoke. It was about all I could manage. I was physically and mentally exhausted from the eighteen-hour drive into the city. I was not sure why he had launched into such an intense subject with me so soon.

Zainab smiled at us from the doorway. "Don't worry, Uncle Fahad. Manal has spent most of her life in America," she said. "She is more American than Arab, even her Islamic side. I had to listen to her sing Nelly's 'Hot in Here' the whole way over."

Then she turned to me and explained. "My uncle is worried you are a Wahhabi or a fundamentalist. The fact that you are coming from America and wearing a veil leads people to assume you are an extremist. Also, many Iraqis are frustrated with Arab talk of insurgents. People like my uncle just want a chance to rebuild Iraq and secure a future for their children. He wants to make sure you are not influenced by Al Jazeera."

"Oh." It was making sense to me. "Don't worry. My Arabic isn't good enough for me to watch Arabic news channels. I would be more worried about my dependence on CNN, which I consider to be MTV for adults."

Uncle Fahad laughed. "You right. All news channels are rubbish. Just *bromise* me one thing. Take time to listen to the Iraqi *beoble*. We suffer a lot, but we are not a *stubid beobles*. We know exactly what we need and what we want. "

His wise words were the cornerstone of proper humanitarian and development work. As much as we thought we knew what was needed, in the end only the communities we planned to work with really knew. That evening I made that promise both to him and to myself: I would keep my ears open and listen to the Iraqi people.

I felt ashamed of all the fear that had engulfed me on the drive to Baghdad. After all, the only danger we encountered on our way into the city had been reckless driving.

I knew that the people of Iraq had suffered a lot: the Iran-Iraq War, the First Gulf War after the 1990 invasion of Kuwait, thirteen years of sanctions, and now Operation Iraqi Freedom. The time had come for the Iraqis to seize their own future. It was long overdue and well deserved.

I felt a rush of excitement at the idea that I could be a part of a positive change, but this was followed by a rush of exhaustion. The time for change was long overdue, but it would have to wait until the next morning. I needed to get some sleep.

* * *

Three days later and five pounds heavier from Uncle Fahad's excellent food, it was time to bid him good-bye. It was hard to leave. Uncle Fahad had reminded me of Iraq's legendary hospitality. Each night we feasted in his garden on traditional Iraqi meals. From kafta (a grilled ground meat and vegetable dish) and kebabs to amazing biryani rice dishes, I could not remember when I had last enjoyed such scrumptious dinners. We would end the night with him smoking on a Cuban cigar and me puffing away at a shisha (a water pipe with flavored tobacco).

My days were filled with excursions to nearby neighborhoods, where I began an initial assessment of community needs in and around the city. I could not have asked for a better guide than Zainab. Her rich experience in working with women in war-devastated areas, coupled with the fact that she was an Iraqi national, made her an Iraqi treasure incarnate. Because we stayed with Uncle Fahad for a few days, we were able to delay being dropped into the whirlwind expatriate life of soldiers, journalists, government workers, and foreign aid workers that was emerging. We were able to experience Iraq in a raw and unadulterated form.

I did not want to leave Fahad, but I knew I could not continue to impose on his warm hospitality. Zainab's trip inside her homeland was short. Her main objective had been to help me get started, and she was due to leave for Amman the next day.

My next destination was the hotel I would call home for the next month. Mark, the logistics officer for Women for Women who had preceded me into the country, had reserved a room for me. He pointed out that by staying at the hotel for a month, we could take our time in scouting out a house for me to rent. We could make sure we found a good place. He was waiting outside Uncle Fahad's with a driver to accompany me to the hotel.

There was still no word on my luggage. I would have to be creative with recycling the three outfits I had bought at

Mansour, an affluent Baghdad neighborhood lined with shops boasting the latest Turkish fashions. I wasn't so worried about my clothes, however. Medication for my back had also been in my suitcase.

Two years before, while horseback riding at the Pyramids in Cairo, I had been thrown off my horse when a donkey-drawn cart came around a corner and startled my horse. The horse reared up, and I fell off. Apparently, the damage from my fall was nothing compared to the damage I did to myself by immediately getting back on the horse and continuing to ride. The result was chronic pain in my lower back. It tends to act up after long trips. I was in desperate need of my muscle relaxant.

Uncle Fahad came out to bid me farewell. "Do not be stranger. Just cause Zainab is leaving does not give you reason to *disabbear* from me."

I promised to stay in touch.

* * *

On the way to the hotel, Mark and I passed my favorite landmark in Baghdad—the statue of Kahramana. Situated in the middle of a traffic circle at the intersections between Karada Dakhil (the inner district) and Karrada Kharij (the outer district), Kahramana was built in the 1960s, inspired by the story of Ali Baba and the forty thieves from *A Thousand and One Nights.* I love the statue for many reasons. The fact that it was built nearly four decades ago was a testimony to the talent of all Iraqi artists. Most impressive of all was the fact that the heroine of the story was a woman. No other Arab country showcases a contemporary work of art that depicts a female heroine in the middle of their streets.

I asked the driver to slow down so I could get a picture, but when I realized there was no water in the fountain, I told the driver to keep going.

When there was water in the fountain, it flowed from Kahramana's jug into a row of forty jugs below. The cascading water gave the statue its grandeur. I did not want a photo of Kahramana without the tumbling water.

Ten minutes later we pulled up to the Sultan Palace Hotel, near Al Tahariyat Square. The hotel was a fusion of Arab, Oriental, and Western designs. The light brown brick building reminded me of Georgetown townhouses. The brickwork stood out in contrast to the rectangular wooden geometric art carvings that marked each floor of the hotel. A red triangular gazebo served as the entrance to the hotel. It looked more appropriate for a Buddhist temple than a Baghdad hotel. The eight-foot-tall wooden doors also incorporated the geometric artwork, a popular Arabesque design, which carried over to the hotel interior.

"Electricity is almost one hundred percent dependent on the hotel generator," Mark said as he handed me my key. " If I were you, I would take the stairs, not the elevator."

Not a problem. After all the good food at Uncle Fahad's, I could use the exercise. My room was on the sixth floor, and by the time I got there, I was completely out of breath. But the hike up the stairs was worth it. The room was spacious, with a television and a small refrigerator. I could ask for nothing more.

Mark had arranged a dinner with some of our hotel neighbors. When I arrived downstairs, I found him with three other men and a woman. He introduced everyone. They were all from a wide range of nongovernmental and U.S. nonprofit organizations. Most of them had arrived in Baghdad a month before. Everyone was nursing a glass of beer.

I ordered a Diet Coke from the bar and was relieved when it arrived. I am addicted to the stuff, and when I lived in Iraq in 1997, Diet Coke had been almost impossible to get. Looking around the hotel restaurant, which was smattered with people from all nationalities, I could see in stark detail that Baghdad was a very different city. In 1997 it would have been impossible to see this kind of diversity outside the UN compound.

When we headed toward the hotel lobby, I began mentally drafting my first mass email to my friends and family. I couldn't wait to describe everything I had seen this week: the city, the women, the program we were starting. Most of all, I couldn't wait to tell them that I had been right all along. Everything was going to be just fine.

Chapter Three

BREAKING THE BARRIERS

Although life in Iraq instantly grew on me, it would be misleading to say I quickly grew on the new Iraq. I desperately fought back the feeling that I was the odd woman standing. It all started when Mark introduced me to our three national staff members.

Without any programs established, our staff consisted only of a local logistics team: Yusuf, Fadi, and Mais. Since we did not have an office space, the first time I met them was in the hotel restaurant. Mark had arrived a month earlier to narrow down our choices of where to base the office. We were to make a final decision in the next few weeks.

The three staffers stood in a line, looking at me as if I had landed from outer space. I reached out to shake their hands. All three appeared to be frozen in place, and then they shook my hand awkwardly and gave me tight, forced smiles. The look of disappointment on their faces was obvious, although I didn't know its source.

I tried to break the awkwardness by asking a few questions. They mumbled answers, looking more annoyed than comforted. Mark must have sensed the tension, and he began to ramble on about the great work that Yusuf, Fadi, and Mais had done over the past few weeks.

I jumped in to try to break the ice again. "Well, that's all good. But at the end of the day it's still a bit odd. Women for Women, and all I see in front of me are four men. We are going to have to change that."

The moment would have been less painful if I had slammed into an iceberg. The three continued to look at me with blank stares. I tried to fumble my way through my awkwardness by reassuring them I was only joking and very much appreciated their hard work. I only made things worse, and for the next few days I felt like a clumsy freshman on the first day of high school. Later I learned that the three men had been promised an opportunity to work with an American woman. Instead, their boss looked a lot like an Iraqi woman.

I drifted out into the hotel lobby, and I could hear the three of them arguing over which of them would get to remain with Mark—the real American.

* * *

The first to take pity on me was Fadi, a twenty-nine-year-old college student studying business and trade at an evening school. He was a Catholic from Basra, a major metropolitan city in southern Iraq. His parents had moved to Baghdad when he was a child, and he had spent most of his adult life here. Since Fadi had to work during the day, he had been trudging through college for the last eight years, although he was now in his final year. His English was very weak, and he was keen to practice with a native speaker.

For the first few days I spent most of my time traveling in Fadi's *Flintstones*-esque car, a battered beige Iranian-made four-door Peugeot. With dents on the side door and hood, it looked as if it had just emerged from a stampede. When I first saw the vehicle, I didn't think it could move. But Fadi reassured me that it was in perfect shape despite its looks. With the Iraqi sun beating down on me, I only had one question: did the air conditioning work? He promised me it did.

We were heading to a meeting in a hotel near the affluent Jadrieh neighborhood to attend a coordinating meeting for a new initiative called the NGO Coordinating Council in Iraq (NCCI). Mark didn't give me much of a briefing on what the meeting was about, but I figured I didn't really need one. It was all in the name. The NGOs were going to try to coordinate their efforts. As I remembered from my experience in Afghanistan, such a simple task was one of the more painful I had endured. I wasn't looking forward to it.

As we drove, Fadi asked questions about my background, and I answered him as directly as possible. He was very lighthearted, and his easygoing style instantly made me comfortable. I found myself opening up to him and telling him about the family drama that had preceded my arrival in Iraq. I could feel his guard coming down as he began to share similar family stories with me. He started playing tapes of famous Arabic singers, asking me what my favorite song was. I explained to him that I hardly listened to any Arabic songs.

"Okay. I have the perfect song that you will definitely know. It is very old." He popped in a tape and an Arabic woman's voice came pouring out over a Spanish beat.

I shook my head and smiled.

Fadi shot me a skeptical look. "Are you telling me you do not know Elissa?"

I chuckled at the disbelief in his voice. It was as if I hadn't heard of the pope. I shook my head again. Next thing I knew, Fadi slammed on the breaks.

"What the hell are you doing?" I asked.

"Where have you been?" Fadi replied as he shook his head disapprovingly. "You don't know Elissa? Where have you been? Even we Iraqis know Elissa. And we have been cut off from the rest of the world."

I instantly bent over with laughter. Not only was he shocked, he was offended. I quickly learned why. Elissa was Fadi's favorite singer, and he had followed her career passionately since she first appeared on the Arabic music scene. She was a big shot in the Arab world and arguably one of the most well-known Lebanese singers. It was beyond his comprehension that I hadn't heard of her. I reiterated that I never listened to Arabic music, that I was more into hip-hop and alternative music.

Fadi launched into a speech about how music was the unifying form of communication across cultures. He asked me to write down my favorite singers. I obliged: Mary J. Blige, Eminem, Sean Paul, Rage Against the Machine, and Nirvana. If music was the great unifier, though, I had a feeling my iPod wasn't going to be much of a bridge.

Fadi pulled up in front of the hotel, his car looking out of place next to the huge white SUVs parked outside. He said he'd be back for me in an hour. The meeting was in English, and since he would not be able to understand what was being said, there was no reason for him to stay.

* * *

I entered the small conference room where the meeting was being held. There were at least fifty people sitting around a group of tables that had been arranged in a square. I looked for a familiar face. There was none, so I sat in the first empty seat I found. I was ten minutes late, and the meeting had already begun. Introductions had been made, and the group was discussing the first agenda item. The chair was proposing a joint letter to the U.S.-led Coalition Provisional Authority (CPA). Since the coalition forces had toppled the former Iraqi government, they were required by international law to provide governance in the interim. Since the CPA was the transitional authority established to govern Iraq, NCCI argued the joint letter should be addressed to them and signed by all the NGOs. Copies of the letter were being circulated.

I quickly glanced through the letter. It was unbelievable. The letter was extremely harsh and antagonizing, not to mention poorly written. It was clearly written by a non-native English speaker. The letter repeatedly referred to an illegal war, invasion, and the CPA as the occupying power. A long list of demands followed. I had no doubt that if the letter were to make it to the desk of a senior CPA official, it would land in the trash shortly afterward.

There was nothing in the letter's content that I disagreed with. In fact, I wholeheartedly agreed with the main message. Iraqis were waiting for the promise of a better life to be fulfilled. They were being cooperative because they believed the CPA would deliver on that promise. The coalition forces were in a race against time to show tangible improvements and thereby maintain Iraqi support. The crux of the promise lay with the U.S. forces being able to improve personal security and public service for the majority of Iraqis. Time was crucial, because the blistering summer heat, which averaged around 110°F, had already begun. The services outlined in the letter—access to food, clean water, and electricity—were the minimum standards. Yet, as written, the letter would probably never be read.

I raised my hand and diplomatically tried to point out the problem. I also offered to help with the rewriting. Immediately, however, the chairman, a Frenchman, shot down my suggestion. "The point of the letter is to be strong," he said. "Those bastards are here illegally, and it is not a choice to make life better, it is their mandate."

I looked around to see almost everyone around the table nodding enthusiastically. Only in a war zone would profanity in a formal meeting seem normal. I shrugged and explained I would not be able to sign the letter as it was currently written.

"Of course you will not. You are an American," he retorted.

"It has nothing to do with my being American. It's because I am a professional," I replied, realizing just how American I sounded. "Like I said, I agree with everything in the letter. I just don't agree with the approach."

I was frustrated with the fact that this Frenchman was so easily dismissing my concerns. He clearly labeled me the moment he heard my accent. I wasn't trying to be an obstacle; I was trying to ensure the letter would have an impact on the decision makers.

An older woman sitting at the back of the room and opposite from me stood up. She identified herself as Margaret Hassan, head of Iraqi operations for CARE, a UK-based humanitarian organization. Margaret reiterated the same point I had been trying to make, and she also emphasized that her organization would not be able to sign the letter as it was. She also offered to help redraft the letter. Although she did not get the same brusque retort from the Frenchman that I received, she did not manage to change their minds.

In the end, the group voted to send the letter with a few grammatical adjustments. The abrasive tone would stay. I was fuming.

* * *

I went out to the parking lot and found Fadi faithfully waiting. He could see that I was upset and asked me what was wrong.

I gave him a quick summary of the meeting. He laughed and told me this was typical. Iraq was divided between people who were pro-war and anti-war, with all Iraqis falling in between the cracks.

I could understand that the world had polarized into the same political divisions, but I was disappointed to see it in the development and humanitarian sector as well. As a relief worker, who could be a supporter for war? But the debate in my mind was moot: the war had happened and people were suffering. Now, what were we going to do about it?

I was angry at the insinuation that my judgment was distorted because I was an American. I also couldn't help but feel irritated that I had been singled out among the group. I had been looking forward to a feeling of solidarity with people who were in the same field. Instead a flippant Frenchman pounced on me.

We began to drive back to the Sultan Palace Hotel. While we were driving, Fadi took the keys out of the ignition and handed them to me.

"Open the *chakmacha*," he instructed.

"How the hell did you do that?" I asked, staring at the keyless ignition and amazed the car was still running. "And what the hell is a *chakmacha*?"

"My car is very special. This is just one of its many tricks," Fadi grinned. He pointed to the glove compartment in front of me. "That is the *chakmacha*."

I opened the glove compartment, and he reached over and pulled out a tape. He popped it into the car stereo. A second later Mary J. Blige's "Family Affair" was blasting.

"I made you a tape," Fadi said, looking very proud of himself.

While I was at the meeting, Fadi had run across the street to one of the many bootleg video and music stores. Based on my list, he had the disc jockey at the store make a mix tape for me.

I was thrilled. It was such a thoughtful gesture. I found myself forgetting about the meeting and grooving with Mary J. Blige. I asked if he liked the music.

Fadi flashed an award-winning smile. "I am Catholeek. How can I not like someone named Mary?"

I laughed. At least Fadi had grown to accept me.

The question remained, would anyone else?

Chapter
four

CHOOSING SIDES

A WEEK LATER I HAD my answer.
No.

Although Fadi had become my new confidant in Baghdad, Yusuf and Mais still treated me with stiff formality. I didn't have much time to worry about team building, though, because my relationship with the other NGOs had grown strained after the NCCI coordinating meeting. I had been labeled as an American NGO. Heaven forbid. Apparently American NGOs were seen to have a different code of conduct than European NGOs.

I couldn't exactly blame them. European NGOs had strict guidelines about entering the Green Zone and working with the Coalition Provisional Authority. Most American NGOs were more relaxed. They were willing to attend meetings in the Green Zone and often went to events hosted by the CPA. The fact that I leaned more toward the European code of conduct and was leery of being associated with the military's purpose instead of women's rights was irrelevant. I was an American who worked for an American NGO. Sides had been chosen by default.

Meanwhile, Mais habitually pulled Mark to the side to complain about my announced policy against interacting with U.S. military. Mais fell into the pro-war camp, the lead cheerleaders for all things American. He repeatedly argued that the Iraqis were in debt to the United States for toppling Saddam and that we should not shy away from interactions with the U.S. military. I tried to turn to Fadi for support, but his area of expertise revolved around the best music, the best kebab, and the best sites to see.

Yusuf stayed on the sidelines. He was a real mystery to me. I tried to engage him in conversation, but he would silently smoke a cigarette and let me ramble on awkwardly.

While NCCI ostracized me for being too American, Mais incessantly labeled me as anti-American. I simply could not win.

At the same time, I wasn't making any friends among the Iraqi women leadership either. I quickly learned not to take it personally, however.

They barely trusted one another.

For thirty years any form of organization in Iraq was considered treasonous, and membership was punishable by death. Few organizations existed underground. Any opposing parties fled to the neighboring countries, mainly Iran. The majority of Iraqis lived in a climate of fear. Their best coping mechanisms had been to avoid the public sphere. Iraqi life was focused mainly inside the home. Even then, Iraqis were not guaranteed to escape the wrath of Saddam and his cronies. Stories were plentiful of families wrongfully accused of treason by a member of the Baath Party intent on a personal vendetta. If you were lucky, you were imprisoned or stripped of your Iraqi passport and driven to the Iranian border.

Most Iraqis were not lucky. They were either publicly executed or just disappeared. Nonetheless, Iraqi families desperately tried to hide in the sanctuary of their own homes. Trust had completely disappeared, and interaction with neighbors, colleagues, and even extended family was often minimized.

The culture of mistrust didn't just vanish the moment U.S. tanks rolled into the streets of Baghdad. In fact, it was stronger than ever. The old style of writing Big Brother reports and informing on those who had anti-Baathist sentiments often led to people's disappearance in the middle of the night—and this practice still continued. The only thing that had changed was the subject line and the recipient. Now the reports were accusations against former Baathists, and they were directed to the U.S. military. These reports often resulted in job dismissals or a midnight visit by soldiers breaking in doors and yelling "Go! Go! Go!"

The dissolution of any form of local government and the lack of grassroots organizations meant that there were no natural counterparts with whom we could work. This was true at all levels, from government institutions to civil society organizations to women's groups. International organizations were dropped into a black hole and forced to navigate the new terrain on their own.

Despite the challenges, local civil society inside Iraq was growing. In fact, it was about to burst at the seams. Within a few months of the announcement of the conclusion of Operation Iraqi Freedom at the end of March 2003, thousands of Iraqis were standing in line outside the Green Zone to declare their membership in nongovernmental organizations. With this mushrooming of NGOs, it was hard to weed through the opportunists to find the real thing.

With Iraqis unable to trust one another, they sure were not about to trust me. In fact, they made it clear they had no idea what to make of me. Since most of the Iraqi women leaders were in their early fifties, they were primarily put off by my age and openly questioned if the best America had to offer to champion the Iraqi women's cause was a twentysomething Palestinian.

I struggled to make myself open to their inquiries. It was extremely difficult to allow them to ask so many personal questions, some of which verged on private attacks. One woman openly questioned how I could say I promoted women's rights while wearing a head scarf, which in her opinion was the epitome of a misogynist interpretation of Islam.

These women were very different from the women I had met in the impoverished areas of the country. In fact, most of these women refused to admit there were any impoverished areas. They argued that poverty existed only in the southern governorates. When I tried to show them photos from Baghdad neighborhoods, they accused me of playing a divisive role among Iraqi women.

"You want us to feel sorry for ourselves," one Iraqi woman activist yelled at me during a meeting of women leaders. "You are trying to make us look like we are Afghan or African women. Well, we are not. We are women of power!"

Another woman added, "You say you come from America, but I never see you with the Americans. How do we know you are not from Iran? You want to make all Iraqi women cover their heads like you do. We love our freedoms, and now that we have got it, nobody can take it away!"

I couldn't decide whether to be impressed by their spirit or insulted by their attacks. I knew that wearing a veil would be a challenge, but I hadn't expected that the only people who seemed to be questioning my *hijab* were the Iraqi elites! I had never before had people so outwardly affronted by my religious dress, and I was having trouble knowing how to respond. I realized that the only way to gain their trust and understanding was to maintain an open and transparent style—no matter how hard some of the Iraqi women were making it.

It was also apparent that they trusted people who wore uniforms. The CPA sponsored a series of workshops and conferences and invited all the Iraqi leadership to attend if they were brave enough to enter the Green Zone. Needless to say this was a small percentage, but they were an impressive group. Doctors, lawyers, and engineers came to the Green Zone meetings, which were often chaired by someone in a military uniform. The fact that I would not attend these meetings spoke volumes to the Iraqi women leaders. If I wasn't there, then I wasn't to be trusted.

Nonetheless, I refused to allow myself to become a darling of the CPA or the U.S. military. The CPA was an extension of the Bush administration, and I strongly believed that the U.S. forces in Iraq would bring nothing but destruction to the country. Despite the enthusiasm for the CPA from many of the Iraqis I encountered, I held firmly to my suspicions. I saw the war as a matter of securing personal gains and interests. It seemed to me that the welfare of Iraqis was the last concern in any U.S. decision maker's thoughts.

The CPA, however, was doing its best to reach out to the international NGOs. I limited my attendance at any coordinating meetings to those that were hosted by the United Nations. The Canal Building, the main UN base, was not part of the Green Zone. In fact, the UN was headquartered in the building in which I had worked six years before. In addition to the UN meetings, many American-based NGOs were also attending meetings regularly inside the Green Zone. Through the U.S. Agency for International Development (USAID), the U.S. government was providing seemingly limitless funds for development programs. They were trying to charge forward in attempting to win the hearts and minds of Iraqis.

I wanted to steer clear of their path. I knew they would use international NGOs as a tool for their own goals. While I lacked the sophistication of the diplomats, I thought my best strategy was to focus on the reason why I had come to Iraq: the women. My efforts would be not be directed toward the elite women who clearly needed no assistance in having their voices heard. Instead, I would focus on marginalized women, the women who had been forgotten under Saddam and who risked being forgotten now.

But the CPA campaign to win hearts and minds was all encompassing. The CPA set up a phone system and provided free and open lines to everyone in the international aid community. This global mobile phone system, the first of its kind to be set up in Iraq, had U.S. prefixes. So people in the United States could call Baghdad for the same price as a national call. As if that wasn't reason enough to head to the Green Zone, outside the convention center the CPA set up a large trailer that housed twenty computer stations with high-speed Internet access. Admittance was granted to anyone with an NGO badge, and within minutes one could be surfing the Internet in air conditioning so strong I dubbed it the "Fridge." Indeed, surfing the Internet was the best way to cool off in Baghdad's relentless summer heat.

The convention center was in the midst of the area in the Green Zone formerly known as "Uday's Playground." Uday, one of Saddam Hussein's sons, had a reputation as a mad playboy. (Saddam's younger son, Qusay, was said to be his father's right-hand man.) Both sons were at the top of the U.S. military's most-wanted list, and Baghdad was full of rumors about their latest sightings.

Uday's Playground included a number of mini-mansions, an underground bunker, the Tomb of the Unknown Soldier, the Al Rasheed Hotel, and the convention center. Between the convention center and Saddam's presidential palace was a large park that included the statue of crossed swords often photographed during the old regime's military parades. In the past, the convention center had been open only to loyalists of the Baathist regime. Now it was the main seat of power for the CPA.

At this point Mark and I still had not found an office, and our only connection to the outside world was via very expensive satellite phones. There were a few Internet cafés popping up in the Baghdad neighborhoods of Mansour and Jadrieh, but the download time was exasperating. It took me thirty minutes just to respond to one email. Not to mention I was often the only female sitting in the midst of young male Iraqi teenagers who were discovering the infinite potential of the World Wide Web. Previously the Internet, like mobile phones and satellite television, had been heavily controlled by Saddam Hussein.

The temptation to take advantage of the speed and comfort of the Fridge was incredible.

∗ ∗ ∗

"Beware of Greeks bearing gifts," I cautioned Mark, who pushed for us to accept the offer of the free phones. Although it would be a godsend on a personal level, I feared our use of the phones and the Fridge would build a bridge of association between the CPA and us. Besides, while it was free to us, someone was paying the bills. If not the U.S. taxpayer, it would inevitably be the Iraqis themselves.

Mark pointed out that this was my call. He also pointed out that we didn't have sufficient funds to use the satellite phones indefinitely. If I decided not to take advantage of the CPA phones, it would mean being completely without any communication.

"Only you see the Americans as an enemy. We do not," Mais interjected. He was in an adjacent room and had overheard the conversation. Mais's English skills were the strongest of my three Iraqi counterparts. He was practically fluent, thanks to Uday's local television channel—*Shabab* (Youth) TV—which played hours and hours of American movies.

Mais had never seen a mobile phone until U.S. troops entered Baghdad in 2003. Denied this gadget for thirty years, he was not about to have his NGO phone taken away now.

"I am not calling anyone an enemy," I explained. " I just want to make sure we remain independent."

"The best way to be independent is to deal with all sides," Mais pointed out. "You cannot ignore the Americans. They are in control of everything. They are the new government. Would you ignore a government, even a government you disliked, in any other country?"

Mais was right. NGOs had been working with hostile governments for decades. They would never dream of refusing to communicate with Khartoum while doing work in Darfur. Even during the time of the Taliban, NGOs coordinated with the Afghan government in order to be able to implement programs. I nodded in agreement—the key was our making sure that we were working with all sides.

"You know what, Mais," I said, " you have a point. I still have my reservations, but for now, your mobile is safe."

Mais looked surprised. He had been poised for a fight. Instead, he smiled and thanked me for listening to his perspective.

* * *

The next few days ran relatively smoothly. I was spending the majority of my time cruising the neighborhoods with Mark and looking for both an office location and a place to call home for the next year. We had to move quickly: in a couple of weeks Mark would leave, and I would be responsible for the entire program.

The precedent for where to situate an office was mixed. Many international NGOs were setting up shop in hotels. Another group rented a row of houses in an affluent neighborhood, with the houses divided between residences and offices. Since the mandate of our organization was to assist the most vulnerable women, I wanted an office in a poverty-stricken area.

The answer to the office location presented itself during one of my quick meetings with Uncle Fahad. His father's old home was in the al-Shawaka district in western Baghdad, and he recommended we take a look at it. The moment I saw the house, I knew Women for Women had found its new national headquarters. The house itself had been abandoned for years, and the wooden door looked like it might fall apart if pushed too hard. Inside, old tiles were stacked in the courtyard. In the middle was an antiquated fountain that no longer worked.

None of that mattered. I could easily see the house renovated in my mind's eye. It was an Ottoman home from the eighteenth century, built in the famous Damascus style, with an open courtyard in the middle of the house. The second floor overlooked the fountain and led to a spectacular balcony with a stunning view of the Tigris River. As I stood on the balcony I could see the fish market to my left and the abandoned British Embassy to my right. Uncle Fahad explained that al-Shawaka had been an affluent neighborhood at the time of the Iraqi monarchy. As a predominately Shia neighborhood that had been loyal to Mohammed Bakr al-Sadr, it had fallen into neglect during Saddam's rule.

Mohammed Bakr al-Sadr was the founder of Saddam's main opposition party, the Dawah Party. He had been executed in 1980. It was common for the Saddam regime to punish disloyalty through institutionalized poverty. By neglecting the maintenance of basic services, Saddam had created many ghettos throughout Baghdad. Shawaka was one such ghetto. Mud homes were built in the backyards of the larger homes, and an open sewer system left streams of waste coursing through the houses.

I took a walk around the neighborhood and was greeted by women covered in black abayas (long black gowns). They stood at their doorways and looked at me curiously. Some extended warm invitations for me to come inside and share a cup of tea. I paused to introduce myself as their new neighbor and promised to visit at another time. Despite Saddam's efforts to destroy the neighborhood, it still displayed strong character, telling the story of its days of glory. Nothing symbolized this better than the old wooden *mushrabiya* (lattice screens hanging from each of the windows). Each of the homes had an elaborately carved wooden *mushrabiya* with glass panes on the other side, giving light and ventilation to the house. They were a symbol of Islamic urban design. They lined the street facing the Tigris River, boldly representing the prosperous status Shawaka residents once enjoyed. I had no doubt that this was the perfect location for our office.

I had to compromise, though…The Shawaka house would not be ready for a few months. In the beginning, I had been adamant about having the office completely separate from my residence. It was difficult enough working in a postconflict environment, and I needed a private space where I could retreat and replenish my energy when needed. Yet I had fallen in love with Shawaka and agreed to have my home temporarily serve as our office until the renovations at Shawaka were complete.

I left Mark to negotiate the details with Uncle Fahad. The action item at the top of my list could be checked off. Awesome office space—found and secured. Now I just needed a house.

Chapter
five

A LOT HOTTER IN HELL

THINGS WERE BEGINNING TO FALL into place. We signed the rental contract with Uncle Fahad, and renovations at the Shawaka office began. I had also identified three provinces—Baghdad, Hillah, and Karbala—where we would begin to recruit women to join the program. I was using the Fridge and the hotel cafeteria as my de facto office. Only one objective remained: finding a woman to work with Women for Women International.

This task was proving more difficult than I expected. There was a wide pool of qualified female engineers, doctors, lawyers, professors, and teachers. They all expressed a keen interest in working to protect women's rights, but they all expressed reservations about working in the ghettoized areas. I needed someone who was not only willing to work in these areas, but who would be openly accepted in these communities.

My search came to an end in the most unlikely of places. I was in Sadr City, interviewing women to enroll in our program. Built in 1959 by Prime Minister Abdul Karim Qassim to deal with housing shortages, Sadr City is one of Baghdad's nine districts. It is considered to be the most impoverished and overpopulated district, with more than one million Shiite residents. During Saddam's regime, the district was further neglected and continued to spiral into poverty. For me, it was an ideal location to recruit women who would benefit from Women for Women's support.

Based on interviews with the CPA-appointed district councils, the local religious and tribal leaders, and the elders in communities, I compiled a list of the most marginalized women in the area. I floated from home to home as part of the enrollment process. In one of these homes I met Muna Hussein. She shared her story with heartbreaking honesty.

Muna had married at the age of sixteen and suffered at the hands of an abusive husband for several years. One day her husband decided he had had enough of her, and he threw her out of his house. She was sent back to her brother's home and forced to leave her daughter and son behind.

"I do not know why he divorced me. I did all he asked. We accepted grief, but grief would not accept us," she said, repeating the famous Iraqi saying. Ten years later, she still had no word of her children.

Muna lived as a modern-day slave for the wives of her four brothers. She was afraid to voice any complaints for fear of being thrown out. She shared a six-by-ten-foot mud house with her brothers and their families. Each brother had staked out a corner and partitioned off their enclave with bed sheets taped across as walls. They shared an outhouse with twelve other families that lived in similar mud houses.

Still, Muna radiated inner strength and confidence. She told me her story as if she were sharing a series of well-known facts, with no self-pity or despair. She described the various jobs she had worked over the last decade in order to make ends meet. As we spoke, I knew that Muna would be the perfect employee. Not only would she be willing to venture into the most shunned neighborhoods, but she was of those neighborhoods. Who better to help me to recruit women?

I asked Muna if she would be willing to work with me. She jumped up from the cushion on the floor where she was seated and hugged me. With tears in her eyes, she nodded enthusiastically. For the next five years, Muna would become the backbone of the organization in Iraq.

* * *

My morning in Sadr City was overshadowed with apprehension about an afternoon meeting I had to attend. As part of my latest attempt to compromise with Mais, I had agreed to go to a meeting in the Green Zone. In the name of convenience, I had been willing to compromise by using the CPA phones and the Fridge. Nevertheless, my attending meetings with the U.S. military seemed to me to be a whole new level of selling out.

Mais could not have disagreed more. He pointed out that although many neighboring countries viewed the U.S. military as occupiers, there was still a dominant group of Iraqis who saw them as liberators. When he realized that argument was getting little traction with me, he struck at my Achilles heel.

The Americans, Mais pointed out, were deciding the future of Iraq. Someone needed to be there to defend the Iraqis' viewpoint. We had spent the last two weeks speaking with marginalized women who would never have access to the Green Zone. During my discussions, they asked questions about their future. Would their sons have jobs? When would electricity be restored? Would the UN food baskets still be distributed? Would their lives be improved?

"Who would give a voice to their perspective?" Mais asked.

Convinced, I agreed to go to the next meeting. Mais was so excited he offered to accompany me even though the meeting would be after working hours.

* * *

Mais and I reached the checkpoint outside the convention center, where all the CPA meetings took place. A soldier asked for our IDs, and we promptly handed them over. Another soldier was sitting on a pile of sandbags. He was wearing dark aviator sunglasses and sipping at his camel pack (a backpack filled with water). He nodded at me.

"Aren't you dying of heat all covered up?" he asked.

"Not really. As far as I am concerned it's hotter in hell," I said with a smile.

"Oh, my God," the soldier with my ID exclaimed. "You speak perfect English."

"Yeah, I'm American," I said nonchalantly.

"Really?" said the soldier with the aviator glasses, standing up. "You know it's safe here. You don't have to dress in a disguise."

"Thanks," I replied. "But I'm good."

"I am sure you are," he said teasingly.

The soldier with the aviator glasses walked over to stand next to the other soldier and took our IDS. "Women for Women. Now that's a great organization. Are you with them as well?" he asked Mais.

Mais nodded, not daring to say anything.

"Well, then, I guess it's only appropriate that you get searched with the women." He pointed toward an Iraqi female translator seated a few meters away. "Go with the incognito American here and get searched."

The Iraqi woman searched me, but she was too embarrassed to search Mais properly. She just patted him on the back and sent us on our way.

Mais turned completely red and murmured about how he had been humiliated. I didn't say anything. After all, it was his idea to be here.

I waited outside the conference room where the meeting was to take place. Everyone was greeting one another and exchanging updates about their work. It was a mixture of uniformed soldiers and Iraqi women. I scanned faces desperate to find someone I knew. Not one person from the NGO coordinating committee was present. I finally saw someone who was recognizable: an Iraqi American who Mark had introduced me to the other night at dinner. His name was Rayyan. He must have sensed my desperation, because he walked over with a sympathetic smile.

"First time, eh?" he asked.

I nodded.

"So, Manal, what part of Iraq are you from?" Rayyan asked.

"I'm not Iraqi," I replied.

"Yes, yes. You are an American. I get it. I am also an American," he said sarcastically with a wink. I could tell he was assuming I was originally an Iraqi.

I couldn't remember which organization he represented. I should have paid better attention when Mark had done the introductions. All I remembered was that Mark had said he was a politically incorrect time bomb with a great heart buried underneath. He had a thick accent that told me he hadn't been in America for very long. His thick black hair and moustache, along with his dark skin, made me suspect he was an Arab. But frankly one could never be too sure. He could have just as easily been Latino, Italian, or Indian.

"No, really, I am not Iraqi. I am originally Palestinian," I replied, deciding to ignore his sarcasm.

"Oh. So what are you doing here?" he asked. He then turned toward Mais to direct the next question. "Your Iraqi boss couldn't find an Iraqi American to fill the post?"

Mais did not answer right away. "Women for Women actually hires on qualifications only. Not nationality. I am sure Zainab never even bothered to ask where she was from."

For no logical reason at all, I felt my heart would burst with pride at Mais's response. It would have been easy for him to just laugh with his fellow Iraqi at my expense. But that wasn't why I was so proud. Yes, he had provided a quick jab on my behalf. But more important, he had refused to be intimidated. And Rayyan was trying to be intimidating.

The meeting focused on creating an incubator for women-led businesses. To me, this was pointless. I couldn't help but wonder where the CPA employees were living. The main request I was hearing from women was for a few more hours of electricity each day. It had been months since the arrival of the coalition forces, and there were still few tangible results.

I endured the first thirty minutes but soon felt the need to say something. After all, that's why I had agreed to come. I shared with them some of the stories of the women I had met and emphasized their need for the basic services of food, water, and electricity. If these basics were not met, then all talk of development and reconstruction was inconsequential.

I had expected the people in attendance to be dismissive. Instead, I could tell they were attentively listening to what I had to say. Afterward, many of them came to me to express agreement with the points I had raised. It seemed that perhaps the meeting had not been a waste of time after all.

* * *

Two hours later Mais and I caught up with Yusuf and Fadi inside the Fridge. I was eager to check my email. Mais was still fuming about the incident at the checkpoint. I could hear him as he told Fadi and Yusuf how the soldier had humiliated him.

"*Saddiq?* (For real?)," Yusuf asked. "Are you saying that you were patted down and body searched by a woman?"

Mais nodded, his face again turning red.

"I can't believe you are complaining," Fadi whined. "I am never that lucky!"

The entire ride back they both continued to tease him and asked him to recount the experience. Just as I noticed we were not heading in the direction of the hotel where I was still staying, Fadi asked if I would like to join them for dinner at his parents' home. His mother had cooked dolma (vegetables stuffed with a rice mixture). It sounded much better than the endless dry kebabs I was getting at the hotel restaurant. I instantly agreed.

I was pleased to meet Fadi's parents. His father was a senior finance manager at Al Rafidan Bank. As a member of the Iraqi Catholic community, he had managed to lay low and off the radar of the Saddam regime. For the last decade Saddam had mainly targeted the Shias and the Kurds. Nonetheless, since he was a native of Basra, he had been denied the right to buy a home in Baghdad. For the last twenty years they had lived in the home of a relative who lived in the United States. I was impressed with Fadi's father and began to ask his advice about the best way to move our program forward. He proved to have great insight and even promised to help with setting up a bank account for the organization.

After the scrumptious home-cooked Iraqi meal, I was served Iraqi tea. It was a great opportunity to get to know better the men I was working with. I felt that my relationship with Fadi and Mais had improved dramatically over the last few days. There had been many chances to interact over the last few weeks, and they had become less formal with me.

Yusuf, however, remained distant. Unlike Fadi and Mais who both possessed the Iraqi trademarks of dark hair and dark skin,

Yusuf had a lighter coloring. With his dirty blond hair cut in a military style, he could have easily passed for a marine. He was much more reserved than the other two, and I continued to find it difficult to initiate a conversation with him. As long as Fadi was around, though, I didn't need to. He seemed to be filled with endless energy and opened one topic after another.

Toward the end of the evening, Fadi asked me what my first impression of them had been. I smiled and told them that I had felt nervous and had a strange feeling that they didn't like me. They looked at each other and laughed, then they just shrugged at me.

"Well," Mais said awkwardly, dragging out the word, "that's kinda true."

I hadn't been expecting them to jump at a denial, but I also hadn't expected them to admit it so openly.

"Look," said Fadi, jumping in, "when we joined the organization, Mark told us an American woman was coming. We were thrilled. We had seen all these blond and blue-eyed women and thought we would have the chance to get to know one. Instead, we got an Arab." He grinned.

"No, that's not it," Mais interrupted. "It's not just that you're not blond, although that was a bit of a shock. It's that you're also covered. I mean, who covers in America?"

"*Kahaltha wa Amaytha*,"[1] Yusuf snapped at Mais. "Sorry, it sounds bad when explained this way. Let's just leave it that we were expecting someone else."

I couldn't help but laugh. I could see their point. Remembering a conversation I had with Zainab when I first arrived, I asked them teasingly, "So you thought I was a fundamentalist?"

"No!" Fadi and Yusuf instantly denied.

But it was too late. Mais was nodding enthusiastically.

---

1 This Iraqi saying means that you have added salt to injury. A literal translation could be rendered, "Trying to put eyeliner on her but blinding her instead."

I laughed again and assured them that I could understand why they were disappointed. I also told them there were more where I came from. There were many Muslim American women who were veiled, gregarious professionals. They were excited to hear about my experiences growing up and pleased to see that I had liberal views despite my conservative dress.

Just as I was heading out the door my CPA phone rang. It was Reema Khalaf, the chairperson of the Independent Nahrain Women's Association. She explained she had received my number from Rayyan and wanted to invite me to a meeting at the Hunting Club.

"I just wanted to tell you I really admired your courage in the meeting," Reema said. "Some of the ladies and I were discussing your points, and we realized, despite your age, you actually have experiences we would like to hear more about."

I put down the phone and smiled. I was growing used to the Iraqi style of throwing out a compliment wrapped in an insult. I had managed to jump over the first hurdle—my age. I looked over at the three men who would help me build the program. The dinner at Fadi's home had been a good idea. I felt closer to them already. And now the phone call from Reema. It looked like things were finally on track.

Chapter Six

HYSTERIA OF HOPE

I HAD BEEN IN IRAQ for less than a month, and all my nonnegotiables had somehow found their way to the negotiating table. That is, I had mentally drafted absolute truths that were to be held sacred. I had drawn theoretical boundaries that were not to be crossed. Yet day after day they were shot down like members of the opposition in front of one of Saddam's firing squads.

I entered Iraq confident that I had my finger on the pulse of the majority Arab and Muslim viewpoint. I could not have been further from the truth. The more I interacted with Iraqis, I saw my crystal clear absolute truths morph into ambiguous disfigured shapes.

In my opinion, Bush's war could bring nothing but death and destruction. Yet instead of despair, the Iraqis with whom I interacted were filled with hopes and dreams for a better future. I had been outraged by the subjugation Iraqis had endured for the past three decades at the hand of Western nations. Yet Iraqis were pointing their finger elsewhere. They openly blamed the Saddam regime for the state of their country. They also blamed their Arab neighbors for having consented through silence to Saddam's tyranny. Many Iraqis went so far as to see the Americans as liberators and defenders of freedom.

My first instinct was that the Iraqis had it all wrong. I cringed with disbelief when I forced myself to watch scenes such as I witnessed in Karbala. I was awed at the sight of the residents of the holy city of Karbala rushing into the streets and ululating with joy as U.S. soldiers passed by. Some of the people held trays of tea cups, offering refreshment to the troops. It was still early in the war, and U.S. soldiers took great pride in stopping to greet the locals and basking in the warmth of a hero's welcome. Something about the picture seemed intrinsically wrong to me. The women were dressed in long-flowing abayas as they, crowded around the soldiers and yelled, "Down, down Saddam! Now Iraq will live!" I forced myself to simply observe and fought off a thousand judgmental thoughts that threatened to flood my mind. Yet the whispers of doubt remained.

What were these women thinking? How could these adolescent boys dressed in desert fatigues, helmets, and bulletproof vests be seen as the heralds of peace? Surely the M16s slung over their shoulders and the pistols bulging at their hips were signs of aggression. How could the Iraqis see the U.S. troops as anything other than occupiers?

But guns had become second nature to Iraqis. There was nothing alarming about them. In fact, they represented the power and strength that was needed. Time and time again Iraqis explained to me that the only way to bring peace was by force.

I refused to be won over. There was nothing good that could ever come as a result of war and aggression. But somehow the Iraqi women convinced me to see the situation through their looking glass. Slowly I began to accept the idea that there might be a successful scenario on the horizon.

* * *

I knew I had taken a dive into the rabbit hole the day I agreed to meet with Joumana. Her story was not unique.

She was one of the thousands of women who had been imprisoned and tortured by the Baathist regime. Joumana stepped forward with a detailed account of her experience. Her story wasn't so much who she was as where she was.

I was called to a meeting at the Al Rasheed Hotel in the Green Zone. The last time I had entered the elite hotel in 1997, I had needed to step over the mosaic tiles that formed George H. W. Bush's face with the caption "Bush Is Criminal." The scene five years later was straight out of Bollywood: the hotel now crawled with U.S. soldiers with George W. Bush as their commander in chief.

My meeting was with Judge Donald Campbell. I came armed with some background information on him courtesy of Google. He was a decorated Vietnam veteran and a retired judge from the Superior Court in New Jersey. Currently, he was a senior advisor to the Ministry of Justice and fortified with the prior experience of reforming a dilapidated judicial system in Haiti under the iron fist of a dictator.

Judge Campbell would be interviewing me to see if I could be trusted to meet Joumana. I was immediately impressed by the man's humble nature. He expressed concern for Joumana and her children, and he was eager to hear my recommendations. My first response was to offer ways to reintegrate her into Iraqi society, mainly through income generation and women's support groups. Judge Campbell shook his head and explained that her situation was beyond reintegration. This wasn't just another woman who had been tortured by the Baathists. This was a woman willing to go on the record. She represented the most sought-after commodity in a country scavenging for evidence of war crimes: intelligence. Joumana was providing names, locations, and details.

The CPA had stumbled upon her courtesy of good old investigative reporting: an article on the front page of the *Washington Post*. The headline A LONE WOMAN TESTIFIES TO IRAQ'S ORDER OF TERROR had caught the attention of top-level government officials from the Potomac to the Tigris. I was told that her stories of torture were verified after a medical examination revealed circular scars resembling the diameter of a cigarette. Other scars indicated she had been tied and even bitten by dogs. The *Post* article had been picked up by a local Iraqi magazine and translated into Arabic. The journalist from the *Post* had used her real name, and the Iraqi magazine had drawn a caricature to accompany the story.

It would not be hard for anyone to find her. Thus it was clear that Joumana was in grave danger.

Apparently, I was not the only one to draw this conclusion. Joumana had friends in high places in the U.S. government as a result of the *Post* article, and an impromptu witness protection program had been formed to protect her.

This included moving Joumana, her mother, and her two children into a trailer behind one of Saddam's palaces inside the Green Zone.

Judge Campbell was concerned for Joumana's psychological well-being, and when rumors that an Arab American aid worker with a women's NGO was in Baghdad, he was eager to make a connection on her behalf. Now that he had met me, he asked if I would like to meet her. Curious, I agreed.

The only person who accompanied me was Yusuf, who was waiting for me at the convention center. This provided great comfort for me because he had proven repeatedly that he was the most reliable of my three staffers. Yusuf was extremely cautious, and he always encouraged me to plan ahead. He was impeccably on time and always completed his tasks right away. Being that caution was contrary to my nature, I found it simpler to have him do that kind of planning for me.

I had assumed the meeting with Judge Campbell would be brief and had set up meetings directly afterward. Yusuf had warned me to block off a few hours since meetings in the Green Zone always ran long. I had scheduled the other meetings anyway, and I didn't have any of the attendees' phone numbers to call should I need to cancel or reschedule a meeting. So I sheepishly called Yusuf and told him I would be another few hours. Naturally, he had all the necessary numbers for my other meetings. He agreed to call and postpone these meetings to the next day. He also reassured me that he would wait for me until I returned.

This was my first tour inside the Green Zone beyond the convention center. I was escorted on a shuttle bus, which was predominately used for the Iraqi staffers who worked in the Green Zone. The workers shuffled onto the shuttle, each one trying to keep some distance from the others lest they be recognized outside the security of the Green Zone.

My escort walked me through the security check point and into the palace that housed the office of Ambassador Paul Bremer. She stopped by the ambassador's office to introduce me to his assistant and some members of his staff. They all expressed personal concerns for Joumana's safety. Judge Campbell's words were still spinning in my head, and I could not shake off a surreal feeling. The view of Saddam's palace and a sea of U.S. Army uniforms was overwhelming. I simply was not able to absorb my surroundings. It was a far cry from the streets of Baghdad, the local restaurants I now frequented, and my tattered hotel on the outskirts of Karrada. This place belonged to a different era. The marble floors were pristine, the gold finishing shouted opulence, and the massive halls represented prosperity. Saddam and his cronies had magically been removed from the stage and replaced by a new set of actors.

Reality only set in after I found myself inside the trailer that housed Joumana. I found her lying on a bed positioned parallel to a side wall. Instantly Joumana pounced off the bed and into my arms.

I was taken aback by her embrace, and she exclaimed in Arabic, "Manal Omar. They told me you would come, but I did not believe them. I did not believe an Arab sister would come to see me. I cannot tell you how happy I am you did."

I was so shocked I could not find any words to respond. I had never met Joumana or even heard of her until an hour ago. Lucky for me a response wasn't needed. Joumana instantly launched into her story.

She was the only daughter of a prominent Assyrian Christian family. They lived in one of the most affluent Baghdad neighborhoods, near Arassat al-Hindya Street. She was spoiled by her parents and was considered one of the most beautiful women in the city. This was not hard to imagine after taking in Joumana's blondish hair and blue green eyes. An Iraqi woman could possess the physique of an ogre and the face of a wicked stepsister out of a Brothers Grimm story but still be considered beautiful simply for her pale skin and fair features. Joumana proudly declared that despite the many men who had courted her, she decided to marry for love.

Joumana turned toward a box that contained her belongings. She pulled out a picture. It was a young and indeed very beautiful Joumana dressed in a red *salwar kameez* draped in gold. In the middle of her forehead was the traditional red dot that symbolized an Indian woman.

"*Naseebi kan Hindi* (My destiny was an Indian)," she sighed. The love of her life was a poor Indian man, and she explained the photo had been taken on her wedding night. Another photo showed her next to a tall, dark, handsome man. She smiled at the photo, and for a moment I thought she forgot I was there.

"I loved him. Although our love destroyed both our lives."

Joumana told me that she had married the Indian man against her parents' wishes and had two children. She smiled as she explained the significance of the names of her children: Saber and Ayoub. She explained that Saber meant patience in Arabic, and Ayoub was named for the prophet Ayoub (Job) who has throughout time represented patience and steadfastness.

"See, from the first day I knew God would test my patience. I knew it because he sent me the hardest man to love in all of Iraq."

Indeed, according to Joumana's story, her marriage brought only heartache, torture, and eventually death for her husband. She explained that their marriage was considered illegal since her husband, despite being born in Iraq, was not an Iraqi. When Joumana tried to use her family connections to get state permission from the presidential family, they were both imprisoned. Joumana was sent to Loose Dogs Prison in Baghdad for two and a half years. Her husband was later released and then imprisoned again and killed.

Joumana was now sitting back on the bed. I was overwhelmed—by the environment, by the story, but most of all by being treated like I was one of Joumana's long-lost kindergarten buddies. No wonder everyone in the CPA felt so protective of her. She spoke with an innocence that made it hard to believe she was a forty-year-old mother of two. She only paused for a few seconds before launching into the story of her own imprisonment. She explained how they raped, sodomized, and tortured her and the other women. She shared the stories of the other women, many of whom were merely teenagers.

"Manal," she said, using my name with such familiarity, "they would tie me to a tree trunk. Rub meat all over my body, and then let loose the damned dogs of that damned Uday. I have marks on my body to prove it," she said and made a motion to take off her shirt. I quickly moved to stop her. There was no need for her to be more intimate than necessary.

I probably would have been in the trailer for hours, listening to Joumana's horrific stories, but we were interrupted by a couple of young soldiers who were bringing Joumana's two children back from swimming in Saddam's Olympic-size pool. Seven-year-old Saber and five-year-old Ayoub noisily jumped into the trailer and ran to hug their mother. They were beautiful children. Their naturally brown skin had taken on an even deeper shade, most likely as a result of hanging out at the pool since moving into the Green Zone.

I watched as the children turned to greet their grandmother. She had been sitting so silently in the corner of the trailer that I hadn't even realized she was there. The grandmother took the pause in conversation as an opportunity to interject her own thoughts on her daughter's situation.

"Binti, my daughter," she said to me. "Please do not repeat my daughter's words. They come at a grave price. Already we are imprisoned in this trailer, and I can only imagine it will get worse. I have begged her to remain silent. But she has never listened to me and insists on dragging all of us to hell."

I felt like telling Joumana's seventy-something-year-old mother that it was too late for that. Her daughter's story was being read all over Washington DC and Baghdad.

I realized the time was getting late and began to bid farewell. I asked Joumana if there was anything she needed. She only had two requests. The first is that I would visit her again. The second was that I would bring her an Arabic Bible. I promised to do my best on both counts.

* * *

There was nothing extraordinary that I could do for Joumana. She had much stronger allies than I. Yet she begged her allies to allow me to visit her in the Green Zone. And I agreed. I was never quite sure why. Agreeing to help Joumana pushed me toward a point of no return. All my attempts to distance myself from the U.S.-led CPA were proving futile. The fact that I was entering the Green Zone on a regular basis meant that I had to cross a virtual picket line of antiwar protesters among the international organizations.

Perhaps I agreed to help because I had just come back from Hillah, where I had visited a mass grave. According to the popular Arabic media, this focus on mass graves was supposed to be an American ploy to shift attention from the missing weapons of mass destruction. But the mass graves were real. And the women tied to the victims were even more so.

The mass graves from the 1990s Shia uprising were only confirmed and exposed after the U.S. invasion. Women flocked to the sites, probing through the remaining items for clues. They searched with grace and dignity for any trace of a loved one, explaining to me that God had answered their prayers by giving them an opportunity to bring closure to their tragedies and mourn their dead. Small piles of nonbiodegradable personal items—a plastic sandal, a wooden prayer bead, shirt buttons—were the only evidence for the women of what had happened...

Joumana's testimony presented an opportunity to have actual hard evidence against some of the perpetrators of these crimes. Judge Campbell had indicated that she was providing details to the authorities, including identifying to U.S. government investigators the sites of mass burials from prisons in Baghdad and the scenes of torture.

I never lost focus that she was one of many. During my trips around Iraq, I conducted numerous interviews with women who believed the end of the dictatorship symbolized a new beginning for them, an end to the era of hopelessness that had enveloped most

Iraqis under Saddam. I met women from all walks of life whose lives began to blossom after the war. They were swept up in a whirlwind of hope, and at some point, I allowed myself to be carried away by it too.

* * *

A week later I sat at the edge of the bed in my hotel room. The first few weeks in Iraq had seemed like years. Each day had dragged on endlessly as I scurried across the country to launch the Women for Women program. On this day I was extremely tired from the day's trip to Babylon as part of a community assessment. I had convinced my driver to make a detour to the ancient site, but I immediately regretted it. It was deeply disturbing to see. The ruins were forced to bear witness as history unfolded, and they often had to pay a price. Saddam had reconstructed the site in a Disneyland-style and had engraved his initials on every brick. The U.S. military presence had taken another toll, leveling parts of the historic site to create a helicopter landing area.

I sat on my bed, my toe poking at a bag as I debated whether my hunger or my exhaustion would win the moment. I was too hot and too tired to have to get dressed and go downstairs to the restaurant. I wanted to stay in my room, where I could relax in shorts and a tank top. Not to mention, my right shoulder was killing me.

I stared absently at the culprit—my emergency bag. I had been lugging around the thing since I had arrived less than a month earlier. I shook my head at the amount of time and research I had invested in the contents of the useless bag. Perhaps it was time to admit that I was being overly dramatic. I could simply keep the emergency bag in my room. There was clearly no need to carry it around every day. With the large generators surrounding the hotel, I had not had any cause to use the flashlight I had packed.

But maybe it could still be put to use. It was probably time to stop hoarding the protein and meal bars I had packed. I fumbled through the bag to find one of the Luna bars. I pulled out the pale blue box holding face masks, a compromise with Mark after fighting with him over whether or not to purchase a Geiger counter.[2] I was convinced I would need one to detect areas of depleted uranium.

That also would probably not be necessary in my new lodgings. I was finally making plans to leave my hotel in Karrada. I had recently found a place near Hay Al Jammah (the university district), where several university faculty members lived. The people who owned the house were part of the extended family of a close friend in Washington DC. The owners were a Kurdish family originally from Arbil, but they had spent the last forty years in Baghdad. In a week I would move into the house. I was excited at the idea of having Iraqi neighbors around a place of my own. I was beginning to feel settled in. I was feeling safe.

As I dozed off while watching reruns of *Friends*, a huge blast jolted me awake. Suddenly the room was dark, the television off. I surmised that the hotel's generator was offline. The blast was followed by a few gun shots. I jumped out of bed and looked for my emergency bag, the contents of which were now scattered on the floor. I quickly pulled on sweat pants, a long sleeve T-shirt, and my *hijab*. I could not decide if I should leave my room, but then the decision was made for me when I heard the sound of rifle fire. The gunfire was very close. In fact, I was suddenly sure the sound was coming from the guards in front of the hotel. That was answered with more gun shots. The shooting slowly became a steady stream of gunfire that got louder and louder. There was an increase in the intensity, and within minutes it seemed like the entire neighborhood had pulled out their weapons and opened fire.

My imagination was back in full force. Certainly the neighborhood had organized an attack on the hotel. Wouldn't that be why I kept hearing the steady shooting from the guards downstairs?

---

2 Geiger counters are used to detect beta and gamma radiation.

Leaving my room was not an option. Neither was staying put and waiting for those who were going to storm the hotel to find me. I decided the best thing to do was to hide. There were not many choices in my hotel room. Under the bed. That would be no easy task for a five-foot-ten medium-build woman.

Just after I managed to play origami with my body parts and squeeze myself under the bed, I heard a knock at my door. It was a simple knock. Not the pounding noise my imagination believed would be more appropriate for the scene unfolding around me. Perhaps I was going to be dragged out by some polite and cordial insurgents. I stayed under the bed. There was another knock. And then someone called my name.

"Manal, are you in there?"

I held my breath. The logical part of my brain was telling me that I knew that voice. It was Mark. Great, my imagination yelled, they have captured Mark, and he has turned me in!

"Hey, all is okay out here. There seems to be some commotion outside. I am going up to the roof to find out what's going on. You wanna come?"

I opened the door, embarrassed by the fact that I was out of breath from my struggle to squeeze out from underneath the bed.

"What the hell?" were the only words I could manage.

Mark smiled. He probably figured that I had panicked. "The news is saying that our troops got Saddam's sons."

"And the gunshots from the hotel guards?"

"Yeah, they seem to have joined in the celebrations. Wanna come up to the roof with me?"

Of course I don't want to go to the roof, you freaking cowboy, was my first thought. But then again, I didn't want to be left alone with my imagination.

I followed Mark. I stopped at the door leading to the roof and watched as he walked out. It looked like someone had set up a huge bonfire in the middle of the sky. Euphoric, celebratory gunfire was arcing everywhere, and I could hear the sound of music and the stomping from impromptu dabke dancing.

I did not sleep that night. Mark and I spent the night shuffling between the roof and the hotel lobby, listening as the Iraqi staff shared an Uday or Qusay nightmare their family had experienced. As I listened to the stories, my thoughts went to Joumana. Where was she now? Had she heard the news? So much of her story centered on Uday and the brutal cruelty of his cronies. I recalled her descriptions of being gang-raped and of the many Iraqi women who lived in fear that they would catch this madman's eye. For these women, justice had finally been served.

* * *

I was scheduled to visit Joumana the next morning. Before I was taken to see her, my escort cautioned me that she had only been informed of the deaths of Uday and Qusay a few hours earlier. They were concerned about her reaction to the news.

When I walked into the trailer, Joumana was pacing back and forth. She turned toward me and smiled.

"Today is my payday," she said. "It is the minute I have been waiting for. It was the vision I held on to every moment I was being tortured. Today, I really believe Iraq will be a new place."

I smiled. Joumana's voice echoed the stories I had heard the previous night. People had described to me how they could no longer remember a time before Saddam's regime. They could not even begin to envision a time after Saddam. Today was a miracle.

Joumana embraced me. "Today, I have decided to allow myself to hope again."

EYES WIDE SHUT

CHARLES DICKENS UNDERSTOOD WAR. "IT was the best of times, it was the worst of times." Over the last three months Baghdad had been divided into two separate cities, each one an unrecognizable stranger to the other.

First, there was the vibrant, cultural city. In that environment, I enrolled in the prestigious Hunting Club in Mansour and went swimming every Tuesday and played Bingo every Friday night. And we ate. Oh, did we eat. Fadi had created a list of the best restaurants in Baghdad, and each night we scratched one more off the list. My favorite was Sasiboun, in Jadrieh, which featured a large outside seating area in the midst of an elaborate British-style garden. We'd smoke shisha there until midnight. Another favorite spot was Arassat Al-Hindia Street in the commercial heart of Baghdad, which was also home to many foreign embassies. The

French restaurant Babiche and the Lebanese restaurant Nabil were among the ones we frequented most. It was a combination of the best of both worlds, East and West. Babiche had several Western-style dishes, including pepper steak and pasta, whereas Nabil was famous for its kebabs, hummus, and the best Lebanese salads.

Yusuf had a list of his own. Although he lived most of his life in the high-end neighborhood of Mansour, he preferred the more common areas. His favorite place was Qadoori at the Bab al-Sharjee market. The market was the electrical hub of Baghdad as well as a haven for criminal activity. That was secondary to the fact that it served the best kebabs in the city. Yusuf preferred restaurants that were frequented by regular Iraqis, and he shied away from the ostentatious Western-style places.

This sentiment was the main thing Yusuf and I shared. I wanted nothing more than to roam Baghdad as a local. We both loved the historic streets of the city, and Yusuf volunteered to be my tour guide. I became obsessed with the vibrant art community that was reemerging. Once a week Yusuf would take me to a string of shops in Karada that housed the work of many local painters. I sipped on cardamom tea as I aggressively negotiated good prices with the shop owners. I took great pride in my purchases and flaunted my latest acquisition at every opportunity.

During this time a fourth male employee joined us. The security situation was fragile, and Mais argued that new employees had to be recruited based on strong relationships. At first, I thought this had been a setup for Mais to hire his brother or cousin. Instead, he brought in a childhood friend, Salah. After I saw how easily Salah integrated into the team, I understood Mais's point of view. The companionship between the four stood as a living testimony of a diverse yet unified Iraq: Fadi was a Christian, Mais a secular Shia, Yusuf a practicing Shia, and Salah a Sunni from the western province of Fallujah. These four men represented different communities in Iraq, and each one introduced me to a different side of Baghdad.

Salah introduced me to my secondary obsession: walking through the markets of Mutanabi Street. Every Friday morning I was ecstatic about taking part in one of Baghdad's oldest traditions: the one-thousand-year-old book market. The main street spread out into alleys, all lined with bookstores. I loved walking down those paths, finding my way into the streets filled with buildings dating back to the Ottomans. Named after a famous tenth-century poet, Mutanabi Street was one of the main reasons I had fought so hard to return to Iraq. The road fulfilled the Arabic proverb: "Cairo writes. Beirut publishes. Baghdad reads."

This was the side of Baghdad I chose to see. My family and friends abroad, however, were reading about the other side of Baghdad. The one that remained quarantined in the back of my mind. The Baghdad that was a stranger to me.

My circle of expatriate friends had shrunken considerably due to several bombings that targeted international organizations. It started on August 19, 2003, when a truck bomb outside the United Nations building killed the top UN envoy in Iraq, Sergio Vieira de Mello. The bombing confirmed many suspicions about Iraq not being safe for civilians. Almost immediately several colleagues evacuated. I had been due at a meeting in the UN Canal Building fifteen minutes before the bomb went off. But I had been delayed at another meeting at Hillsdale, a recently discovered ad hoc camp of displaced Iraqis from around Baghdad. The attack was followed over a month later by a bombing of the International Red Cross. The Al Rasheed Hotel, which had been considered one of the safest places in Baghdad, was then hit by two mortar attacks.

In fact, one evening a mortar round came flying by and landed in the garden of the restaurant next door to Sasiboun as we puffed on our shishas. Yusuf quickly pulled me to the ground, and we laid face down as a second mortar shell whistled by. Once Yusuf determined all was clear, we returned to our shishas.

The saga of Kalthoum wasn't that easy to shake.

* * *

I listened to five U.S. military policemen debate about whose home state had the best beach when Munther, an Iraqi police offer, entered the room. In my opinion, Kitty Hawk had nothing on Myrtle Beach, but Munther interrupted my thoughts and handed me some dates. Time to break my fast.

It was the middle of the holy month of Ramadan, but instead of being at home, I was stuck in a police station with the angry mob of Kalthoum's family waiting outside. I stared absently at the dates, realizing that if it was time to break my fast, the sun had set. The citywide curfew imposed by the coalition would be in effect in less than an hour, and I would be stuck at the police station.

"*Jazak Allahu khair*," I said to Munther and accepted a bottle of water from one of the MPs. As I ate the dates, I scanned the room to see if there was a place for me to make my prayers. Something about bending and prostrating in the room seemed intrinsically wrong, but all the other rooms at the police station were filled with soldiers or Iraqi police. The only less crowded room was the kitchen, where I had first met Kalthoum.

Kalthoum was sound asleep on the bench adjacent to where I was sitting. The past few hours seemed to confirm her story of having been led into drugs; it was clear from her vomiting, sweating, and shakiness that she was going through withdrawal. Or perhaps those were attributable to her pregnancy.

Over the last few hours I had successfully entered my own state of denial. I knew there was no way out of the police station, and if I were to give proper attention to my circumstance, I would probably launch into a full-scale panic attack.

Yusuf and Mais were sitting in a café one block away, patiently waiting for my call to say that the coast was clear. I realized that, with the curfew, they would not be able to wait much longer. I also realized that there was no way in hell I was going to spend the night in this police station. I had boasted in my emails and phone calls back home that I had survived four months in Iraq without having to take any serious risks. But the time for risk taking had arrived.

"Guys, I have to leave," I said turning to Tom, the MP who had initially greeted me when I first arrived.

"Sorry, ma'am, no can do. It's not an option with those Iraqi men standing out there. Best option you have is to hope they are gone in the morning."

I turned to Munther. In all Arab cultures it would be unacceptable for a woman to spend a night in this environment. If word were to get out that I had spent the night at an Iraqi police station—with U.S. military police to boot—it would vaporize my credibility in the neighborhoods. I was confident Munther fully understood what was at stake.

"The other option," he said, "is to wait until after the curfew. These men will not risk staying after the curfew. Once they leave, then you can head home."

I didn't wait for Tom the MP to answer but quickly dialed Yusuf and Mais to see if they were willing to wait for me. I knew they would be taking the real risk. Stories abounded in Baghdad about those who broke curfew. I'd heard about desperate fathers-to-be driving their pregnant wives to a hospital at midnight and getting their cars riddled with bullets in the process. Most likely, we would be stopped at a military checkpoint. Checkpoints were unpredictable. Sometimes after curfew, soldiers would wave you through. Sometimes they would take everyone in the car in for questioning. Often those taken in by the authorities just disappeared.

Despite protests from Tom and the other MPs, Munther promised to escort me outside once the family had left. I bid farewell to Kalthoum, who was only half-awake. Munther shook his head disapprovingly as I promised to be back the next day.

I had managed to broker a peace between Tom and Munther by promising to follow up with Kalthoum the next day, but I knew it would not last long. Kalthoum's staying under the protection of the MPs was a short-term solution only. I needed to find her a safe place.

Munther delivered me to Yusuf and Mais, and we drove home in silence, muttering prayers in the blessed night of Ramadan. Driving late at night in Baghdad generally ended in one of two opposite extremes. In our case, we were thankful that our trip was anticlimactic.

* * *

I woke up before the dawn prayer for Sahoor[3] and could not get back to sleep. I forced myself to wait a few more hours to call Mais and Yusuf. Then I begged them to come to my house as soon as possible. When they arrived thirty minutes later, Mais could not hide his frustration that I had called him again to address Kalthoum's situation.

"It's 7 a.m. It's Ramadan. Even the U.S. soldiers are not riding their translators like this!"

I could do no more than mumble an apology. I knew Mais was right. I was expecting too much from them. In addition to all the extra hours of work, they were taking an enormous risk by being associated with Kalthoum, a prostitute.

"You need to rest. If you keep working at this pace you will collapse," Yusuf interceded.

I was touched by his obvious concern. Yet time was against me, and I knew I had several visits to make before I would be able

---

3   An early morning meal before beginning the daily fast during Ramadan.

to even begin to think of a solution for Kalthoum. The first stop would have to be the conference center. I had befriended a Czech aid worker who had been appointed by her government to help document human rights abuses under Saddam's regime. Ivana was among the few people in the CPA who actually had experience in working with civil society. Although there was little she could do within the CPA, I knew she would at least be able to point me in the right direction. I also knew that by 8 a.m. she would be wide-awake and on her third cup of coffee, having already smoked half a pack of Marlboros.

I hurried through the several checkpoints into the convention center and toward the transitional justice office where Ivana worked. Sure enough, she was sitting in a fog of cigarette smoke, puffing away as she violently shook her head back and forth at the twentysomething U.S. assistant assigned to her. When she saw me hovering at the door, she waved me in as she simultaneously waved her assistant out.

The best part about Ivana was that I would not have to waste time with polite conversation. I had not seen her in two weeks, but I knew I could jump right into the business at hand without her being offended. Ivana recommended I touch base with the Ministry of Labor and Social Affairs. The fact that Kalthoum was under eighteen placed her in its jurisdiction. Legally, the ministry was required to provide her with a place in one of the public orphanages. Ivana explained that would be the best long-term solution because the orphanages were well established and provided a high school education with an option for college. At the same time, orphans in both Iraqi and Muslim society have a special reverence. Numerous verses in the Koran and sayings from the prophet Mohammed (peace be upon him) called for respecting, caring for, and providing for orphans. This would help combat any previous stigma that might be attached to her, and it would provide an opportunity for her to start a new life. Ivana warned me, though, that this option might not work, and that as I reached out to the Iraqi ministry, I should also explore the option of the U.S. military's civil affairs unit.

I walked out of her office on a high. It was a perfect solution. I went back to the car and found Mais and Yusuf had reclined the front seats and fallen asleep. I tapped on the window and tried to offer a grateful smile. As I climbed into the backseat, I explained the plan to them. One laughed and the other snorted. They were not the least bit impressed.

"I will cut off my right arm if the minister does not throw you out," Yusuf said as he chuckled.

"I will cut off something far more important if the minister even agrees to see her," Mais said with snort.

"It doesn't hurt to try," I snapped back, a little hurt and very defensive. I still thought it was a good idea. "Besides, Ivana has already arranged an appointment for me with the deputy minister."

I decided to ignore the skeptical looks the two shot at each other and settled in the backseat to prepare my case for the minister. I knew I would not be able to lie about Kalthoum's background. But she had a compelling story, and the fact that she had been forced into marriage at such a young age solidified her status as a victim. Besides, she was only sixteen years old. The deputy minister had to take pity on her situation.

One hour later it was clear that this was not going to happen. The deputy minister was visibly insulted that I had the audacity to bring such a case to his attention. I tried every avenue to convince him that Kalthoum was not a lost case, that he shouldn't be so quick to throw her to the wolves. Yet he was steadfast in his decision, and he dismissed every argument I brought forward. When I tried to point out that she was underage, he countered with the fact that she was a married woman, which placed her in the category of adulthood. Orphanages were for children only. I tried to argue that she had been forced into marriage at the age of thirteen, which was illegal according to Iraqi law. He shook his head, pointing out that it was a common occurrence during the years of UN sanctions.

"How else were parents to secure their daughters?" he asked.

After sixty minutes of arguing with him, I threw up my hands and tried a different approach. Long ago I had learned that the damsel-in-distress strategy often received quick and candid results.

"Sir, I am at my wit's end. I cannot think of anything else to do. All I know is that I have a problem. Can you help me with the solution?"

The deputy minister leaned forward. He shook his head and then leaned back into his chair. "Do you really want to know what the solution is?"

I nodded.

"Let the natural process go forward," he said. "Her father is the person to decide what will happen to her. If it was my daughter, I would want the same."

"But we both know her father will most likely kill her."

"The problem with you Americans is you ask the questions, but you do not want to listen to the answers. Again, if it were my daughter, I would want the same."

I could not accept his response, but all my phone calls to Iraqi women's organizations resulted in dead ends. Kalthoum was too much of an extreme case, most of them argued. We cannot help her without making ourselves vulnerable to verbal and physical attacks.

I was not surprised by these responses.

* * *

A month earlier I had come across two sisters, ages fourteen and sixteen, who had been kidnapped and raped by a local gang. The two girls knew their attackers, and the Iraqi police carrying out the investigation interpreted that to mean they were complicit. The girls were from a poor neighborhood in southern Baghdad. Before the fall of the regime, one of the neighbors had asked for the sixteen-year-old's hand in marriage. The mother had refused, hoping that her daughter would be able to complete high school.

Shortly after the invasion of Iraq, the boy gathered some of his thug friends and stormed the woman's apartment. He dragged both sisters out by their hair and took them to a private place. The boy raped the sixteen-year-old but argued to keep the fourteen-year-old "intact" so they could sell her at a higher rate. According to the sixteen-year-old, this led to a violent exchange between the two thugs that resulted in their shooting each other. She took the opportunity to escape, but she was forced to leave her sister behind. Three days later the fourteen-year-old was dropped off in front of their building. She had been raped and was in need of medical attention. The gang warned that they would be back to kill them if anyone tried to turn them in to the authorities.

What the gang didn't know was that the authorities were not interested. The local police insisted that the girls had a link with the gang and refused to offer any assistance. The young girls' mother could not afford to move out of their apartment, and the three lived in fear that the gang would be back. Not only was finding the girls a safe haven difficult, but even getting them examined by a gynecologist proved impossible. In most cases in Iraq, forensic officers conducted examinations of rape victims because gynecologists feared repercussions from the family if they confirmed a girl had been raped. In some cases, after hearing the news, angry fathers or brothers had executed the gynecologist.

I had spent days speaking with women's organizations who explained that the sisters' situation was too volatile to tackle. They argued that taking in rape victims would make the organizations vulnerable in their communities, and any woman who was associated with the organization would receive a bad reputation.

There was only one organization in Baghdad at the time willing to take the risk. The Organization of Women's Freedom in Iraq was founded by Yanar Mohammed, a Canadian Iraqi activist. Yanar herself had already received many death threats for her liberal views since her 2003 return to Iraq, and I had visited her office during my first weeks in Baghdad to determine what protections she had to offer women in need. Indeed, she was one of the only women who had built an intricate and highly secure underground shelter for cases like that of the raped sisters.

I tried to offer the sisters the option of going to Yanar for help, but they refused. Yanar was perceived as a controversial figure, painted within mainstream Iraqi society by women and men alike as a leftist feminist who hated Islam. The mother and her daughters feared that being associated with the Organization of Women's Freedom would forever seal their excommunication from Iraqi society. Instead, the mother opted to take her chances and stay in her small apartment. Her plan was to lie low long enough and pray the gang would forget about the incident.

Somehow I managed to convince her to allow the sixteen-year-old to enroll in the Women for Women program. The first day, through tears, she shared the story of her rape with the women in her circle. A safe space had been created where she was able to share her trauma. Most of the women were older than she and instantly took on protective roles. They provided her with emotional support for the following three months. After that, she stopped coming. I visited her home on two occasions afterward, but her mother made it very clear she did not want her daughter to continue in the program. One of the trainers suspected they had received a death threat. The next time we went to visit, the mother and her daughters had vacated the apartment.

* * *

From the moment I saw Kalthoum in the police station, I knew that helping her would not be easy. If helping two teenage girls who had been kidnapped and raped had been so difficult, I could only imagine what helping a married, pregnant teenage prostitute would be like.

I knew I would have to pressure the deputy minister to provide me with a solid option. In the end, I used a wild card Ivana had told me about. Several international agencies such as USAID and the World Bank were poised to provide large grants to the Ministry of Labor and Social Affairs for the purpose of helping marginalized groups. I pointed out that the deputy minister's lack of cooperation could be an obstacle to the ministry's receiving the grants if word were to get out that he was refusing to help the most vulnerable people in Baghdad.

The deputy minister responded with a compromise. He set up an appointment with the director of one of the orphanages for girls. If I could convince the orphanage director to take the girl, the ministry would not object.

It was as good a compromise as I was going to get.

I had to fight back tears of anger as I got back into the car. The deputy minister's answer angered me as much as his arrogance, his passing judgment so quickly on a sixteen-year-old girl.

Fortunately, the director at the girl's orphanage was much more sympathetic than the deputy minister. Yet Asma's answer was the same. She could not accept Kalthoum in the orphanage. She candidly explained that the benefactors of the orphanage would be upset if they learned that Kalthoum was not a virgin. Her being in the orphanage would be seen as an attempt to corrupt the younger girls, and overnight every girl in the orphanage would be labeled a prostitute. Asma explained she had seen many cases such as Kalthoum's, and it deeply saddened her that the state could provide no real solution. She believed it not only failed the individuals but the families as well. In most cases, the fathers would happily relinquish responsibility to the state. But since there was no place to put them, they often had to bear the responsibility and shame themselves. More often than not, the solution was an honor killing.

Asma stated that without even meeting Kalthoum, she was sure the girl would not keep her past a secret. In fact, in the beginning she would probably brag. I did not argue. I knew she was right. Asma walked me out to the front door and reiterated that she was sympathetic toward Kalthoum, but she could not risk the reputation of the three hundred girls under her care.

Before I left I asked her, "If you know the need is there, why don't you fight to create something for these girls?"

"Manal, you need to understand that we are tired of fighting," Asma said. "That's all I have been doing; it's all my mother did. We don't want to fight anymore. It doesn't mean we have given up. Far from it. It just means we want to find a more peaceful way to live something that may resemble a normal life."

* * *

I sat in the backseat of the car. It was now almost noon, and I was nearly comatose from a lack of food and water. Yet I was nowhere near ready to give up. The clock was ticking, and by the end of the night I would need to go back to the U.S. MPs and Iraqi police at the Karada police station knowing that I had a place to relocate Kalthoum.

"Why is this your problem?" Yusuf asked. "I don't see anyone else in this country running around the way you are. You tried. Can you please call it a day and go home?"

A part of me wanted to lean over and smack him. It was the part of me that knew he was right. But I had not tried all the avenues

I knew to resolve Kalthoum's situation: the director of the girls' orphanage had given me another solution. It was one I was not very happy with, but it was a potential solution nonetheless. Asma explained that, in the hierarchy of orphanages (yes, even orphanages apparently have a standardized hierarchy), the bottom of the food chain was the special-needs orphanage. She suggested that my best bet was to take Kalthoum there. She knew the director. Although he was on an indefinite leave of absence, he still called the shots. Asma had called him and made the necessary arrangements. All I had to do was to deliver the news.

"Yusuf, I am not comfortable with the solution she has given me. It feels like a cop-out."

"But you have tried everything," he said. "They all should be grateful you even came up with something. I know I am utterly amazed. It may not be the best solution, but it is a solution."

I knew he was right, so I told Mais to head back to the police station. As we came nearer, Yusuf handed me a bag.

"Put these on," he instructed.

The bag had a long black abaya and flat black shoes. It also had a compact mirror and a makeup kit with a bronzer and a brush. Yusuf smiled and told me to bronze myself so I wouldn't stand out so easily. He also pointed toward my black MBT sneakers and said that they were a telltale sign that screamed American woman. He suggested I wear the flat shoes. I smiled at Yusuf, pleased with the disguise kit he had put together for me.

When I entered the police station, Munther seemed the most pleased to see me, but Tom the MP was a close second. They both rushed toward me and asked the same question in two languages: what are we going to do with Kalthoum? I explained Asma's solution. Both Tom and Munther looked skeptical but shrugged their shoulders. They probably reached the same conclusion I had: there were no real solutions.

As always, Yusuf had planned ahead and produced a disguise kit for Kalthoum too. Dressed in abayas, she and I slipped out the back door of the police station and headed toward Yusuf's car. Before I left, I thanked Munther and Tom. I knew they both had taken professional and personal risks by allowing Kalthoum to stay overnight in the police station.

"I just want you to know that you two probably saved her life," I told them.

Munther nodded. Tom smiled and gently touched my arm. "I want you to know," he said, "you just gave me my answer when my grandchildren ask me what I was doing in Iraq."

I smiled at the two policemen, pleased at the new alliances I had just made. Naturally at that moment I was not thinking of the future, but it turned out that these new alliances would come in handy.

The orphanage for special needs was a disaster. The entire orphanage was in chaos, and the young children had been left with little or no care. Children were lying in their own urine in unmade beds, and each room contained at least thirty beds. There were only three wheelchairs, and the majority of the children needed wheelchairs for mobility. Worse yet, the caretakers were obnoxious and rude and openly gawked at Kalthoum and me, black abayas and all. I could not bear to leave her, but I also knew I had no other choice.

I turned to Yusuf for advice, as he was the only one willing to come into the place with me. Mais had abandoned all hope in talking sense into me, and although he accompanied me on my expeditions, he refused to get out of the car.

Yusuf shrugged and muttered that the call was up to me. Every bone in my body urged me not to leave Kalthoum. Yet I knew I had put Mais and Yusuf through enough. Sunset was only a few hours away, and I could not bear the idea of breaking fast yet again in a police station or, worse, on the street. They deserved to break their fast at home. I deserved to break my fast at home.

"Let's go," I said. I hugged a silent, weeping Kalthoum and told her I would come back first thing the next morning to check on her.

Five minutes after we drove away I began to cry. Perhaps it was exhaustion or hunger or the brutal summer sun. I felt completely beat. Yusuf pulled over, and Mais turned to look at me with a mixed look of sympathy and worry.

"We cannot leave her," I said through my tears. "It's just wrong."

Mais slapped his hand to his forehead. "I knew this wasn't going to be over," he muttered.

Yusuf said nothing. He turned the car around and headed back to the orphanage. There, he instructed me to stay in the car, and ten minutes later he brought out a grateful Kalthoum. She entered the car and hugged me and then tried to kiss Yusuf's and my hands to demonstrate her gratefulness. I could not stop crying, especially as I realized I had almost left her there to be raped or worse.

This nightmare was getting worse. There was no place to take her, and although Yusuf and Mais were willing to help me, they both refused my proposal to have Kalthoum stay with me. I knew it was impossible. I no longer lived at the hotel, and bringing Kalthoum home would compromise all my work with Women for Women International. Not knowing where else to go, we headed toward the convention center in the Green Zone. Ivana had already said that the U.S. military might be Kalthoum's only viable option.

I had no clear plan, but I was not yet in despair…An hour ago I had a clear plan in my mind, and it proved to be the worst idea yet.

I went in search of Capt. Anne Murphy. Erik, a friend who worked with USAID, had connected me with Anne. He said it was a chemistry experiment. "I introduce chemical X to chemical Y and let the chemistry do its work," he explained. Anne and I shared a passion for women's issues, and neither of us knew how to say *no* or *can't*. Erik believed we would make an ideal Baghdad dynamic duo. As I glanced over at a grateful Kalthoum, I could not think of a better situation in which to put his theory to the test.

It was difficult for me to turn to the U.S. military to help Kalthoum, but I had been slammed against a wall and given little space to maneuver. I needed to buy time.

With her quick, action-oriented response, Anne did not get caught up in the details. She understood I had a young woman who needed a place to stay, and she got to work to see where she could place her. Within an hour of our arrival at the convention center, Anne had convinced a female sergeant who had been assigned a trailer to take Kalthoum with her. It would be a temporary solution, no more than three days. But it just might buy me the time I needed to figure out what to do next.

* * *

That night Yusuf insisted I come home to meet his family. He argued that I had been breaking my fast on junk food for the past week, and I had earned a home-cooked Iraqi meal. With the sun setting and my stomach growling, I was in no condition to argue with him.

Yusuf boasted to his family how I had refused to give up on Kalthoum, which secretly pleased me. I was surprised, though, to see that he took pride in his work of helping women. His mother would gasp, "*Ya Allah*," at his description of every turn of the day's events and then wag her finger at me, telling me not to get her son into any trouble. She had been a school teacher, and she had a smile that reached her eyes. Her laugh seemed to come from deep within her body, and it carried a sense of compassion and tenderness. I liked her instantly.

I also met Yusuf's older sister, Maysoon. In the beginning, I felt uncomfortable with the way she looked me over from top to bottom, as if she were doing a thorough psychological scan. But within the first hour we were chatting like high school friends, comparing our likes and dislikes. When Maysoon's husband, Hussein, came to pick her up, I was disappointed that she had to leave. Hussein agreed to stay another hour, and he joined the family in outlining their personal history for me.

Hussein was a man of few words but enormous presence. Originally from the district of Khadamiyah, he belonged to a wealthy merchant family, and his family owned land all across southern Baghdad. I was impressed by his humble nature. He insisted on working his own land and managing his business firsthand. He had hundreds of employees, but from his deep five-o'clock shadow and the bags under his eyes, I was willing to bet none of them worked as hard as he did.

I had no idea then that Maysoon and Hussein would become dear friends, that I would visit them often in their home and became a de facto aunt to their two children.

After an amazing meal, Yusuf drove me home. We rode in silence, and I allowed myself to get lost in my thoughts about the day's events. I was stuck on the phrase Asma, the director of the women's orphanage, had used. *We are tired.* During my six months in Iraq I had met with women from a wide range of backgrounds. Although their circumstances were different, they all had in common the fact that they wanted to share their stories. And a common thread in those stories, a thread repeated in almost all my interviews with Iraqi women across the country, was that idea. They were the words that bridged the gap between rich and poor, literate and illiterate, and ethnic and religious: *ta'abna* (we are tired) and *malayna* (we have had enough).

In their hearts, these Iraqi women believed their pain and suffering were finally over. Perhaps they believed so strongly that, through a process of mental osmosis, I came to believe it too. I refused to see the dangerous scenarios I was entering and remained focused on the micro level. My strategy was to remain focused on the individuals in front of me. I convinced myself that if I could help one, two, perhaps even ten women, then I had fulfilled my role. I had become so focused on maintaining an optimistic viewpoint that perhaps I had lost perspective.

Chapter
Eight

A PLACE OF FANTASIES

As I allowed myself to become more optimistic, I noticed
a shift in attitude toward me from the Iraqi women. My
pessimism had been creating a barrier between me and the very
women I was trying to help. They had enough negativity in their
lives. They were looking for someone to join in their dreams for
a better future. Once I opened myself to their stories, I understood their desire to compartmentalize their traumas as a thing
of the past.

I became convinced that the debates over weapons of mass
destruction or the legalities of the war were irrelevant. The fact
remained that the war had happened, and the ultimate price would
be paid by the Iraqi women. They refused to be passive spectators.
No matter what socioeconomic background the women were from,
they were all struggling to survive and create a better future. I was

determined to do everything I could to make their lives better, no matter what the cost.

But here I was, months past my arrival in Baghdad, chasing down deputy ministers and directors of orphanages, mediating between U.S. MPs and Iraqi police sergeants, and still failing to provide any real solutions. The rhetoric on helping women was abundant, but the reality was scarce. I realized I was attached to doing work through traditional humanitarian means. I was looking for local solutions, forgetting that for more than thirty years all local initiatives had been met with an iron fist. Any past efforts to organize had been thwarted by the Baathist regime. Anyone who demonstrated leadership in the community was killed, went missing, or was dropped off at the Iranian border.

I had been so reluctant to look at the U.S. military as a feasible option that I was willing to put a teenage girl's life in danger.

Anne Murphy had proven she was a woman of action, and she helped me with little hesitation. I had heard of another woman of action who worked for the Coalition Provisional Authority in Hillah. Her name was Fern Holland, and I had met her briefly during my visits to Karbala and Hillah, the provinces south of Baghdad.

Fern impressed me. She was one of the few U.S. civilians who took the time to meet with the local authorities and who spent endless hours listening to women. Initially Fern was hired by USAID to run its programs supporting democracy in governance. By January 2004 she was hired by the CPA's office in Hillah to continue the programs with women's groups. Fern convinced the CPA to provide a multimillion-dollar grant to open up women's centers in the southern governorates.

She invited me to a conference in Hillah that would focus on the status of women in Iraq. The conference was already making waves across the women's organizations, and there was a rumor that Condoleezza Rice was planning to attend. For most people that rumor was a huge incentive. For me, I was concerned that the Iraqi women's movement would be linked with the American occupation. The conference's close proximity with the military could have a strong backlash. Even as I explained to Fern that I would not attend the conference for fear of being associated with the military, I could feel my conviction beginning to dissipate. The word circulating among the Iraqi women was that Fern had the power to make big changes. They were eager to be by her side.

I knew the time had come to expand my comfort zone once more. I had been eager to delay the inevitable moment of having to turn to the U.S. military for assistance. With Kalthoum, that moment had come. Despite my good intentions, I had been just as helpless in aiding Kalthoum as I had been at providing support to the two sisters who had been abducted and raped. Perhaps the missing ingredient to finding more practical solutions was finding more action-oriented people who had the power to make decisions. I needed to expand my circle of allies…I knew then that I was willing to push my security limits in order to stay in Iraq. The international community had abandoned the people of Iraq many times before, and I could not bear to see it happen again.

* * *

Over the next few days I learned to navigate the Green Zone. Previously, my only entry had been for specific purposes: to visit the Fridge or attend women's coordination meetings and meetings with Iraqi government officials. Now my visits were daily.

After a week of nonstop meetings inside the Green Zone, I began to refer to it as Disney World. It was a place of fantasies. The majority of people living inside the Green Zone did not travel outside except for brief missions. These missions often included military escorts or armed guards. Those who dared to venture for quick visits outside of the Green Zone were revered as experts on the country. The walls surrounding the Green Zone began to represent the metaphysical walls between the United States and the Iraqi population, and these walls were becoming more and more apparent every day.

Translators played a central part in maintaining the fantasy. They seemed to fall into three camps. First, there were the translators who were working because they desperately needed the income. They had no strong political affiliation and were there for a paycheck. Second, there were the idealists. Their desire to help form a new Iraq was naive yet inspiring.

Third, there were the opportunists.

Opportunistic translators were a nightmare for me every time I passed through a checkpoint. Over time I learned to spot these translators a mile away and would automatically prepare to present my U.S. passport. They were often seated in the midst of the soldiers, perched on the edge of their chairs, ready to pounce on the next person to cross over. They tried to imitate the accents of the soldiers, which often came out as a mix between a New York cab driver and a Texas rancher. Many times I had to bite my tongue whenever an Iraqi translator seemed to purposely stir up trouble. Often they would make inappropriate comments about the Iraqi women standing in line. Sometimes they shot off antagonizing questions to the Iraqi men, further reminding them of their weakness as they stood in line in their homeland at the mercy of the Americans.

During one of my visits to Kalthoum, I witnessed one of these incidents and could not keep my mouth shut.

"*Indaaree* (turn around)," one of the young soldiers instructed. This was during a time when U.S. soldiers believed that imitating local Iraqi slang was cute. Iraqis saw it as the soldiers' attempt to be sensitive to the local language and culture. Very soon the same words were interpreted as mocking, and that infuriated the Iraqis who had to pass through the checkpoints. Indeed, the soldiers' use of local words and phrases would change, but that hadn't happened yet.

As I was being searched at a checkpoint, an older man cut through the line. He looked like he was in his late sixties, and he was sweating from having to wait in the heat. I smiled at him. He looked like a sweet old man, and his gray hairs and slight slouch reminded me of my grandfather.

He smiled back while quickly apologizing for cutting in line. He explained in Arabic, "My sons, I do not want entry. I am an army soldier and was told salaries are being distributed. I am just coming to ask where I need to go. Please, my family has no money except this salary."

An Iraqi translator jumped up and started yelling at the man in Arabic to get back. The old man looked startled. The translator continued to scream and gesture dramatically, which made the American soldiers nervous.

The young soldier looking through my bag jumped up and pointed his rifle at the old man. "What is he saying? What is he saying?" he screamed to the translator.

"He say he military officer. He threaten me. I tell him stop," the translator shot back. As soon as they heard the words *military officer*, the four American soldiers raised their rifles at the old man.

Likewise, the old man's sweetness evaporated. He could not understand the translator's English words, but from the guns being pointed at him, he knew the words were hostile. His body automatically straightened, and his voice hardened.

"I do not want trouble," he said. "I am asking for my right. Can you help or not?"

The translator responded with outrage. "*Inta makhabal?* (Are you crazy?)," he asked and waved his arms frantically. "Do you know who you are speaking to?"

The heightened tension was unnerving. I noticed Yusuf step back and wave for me to do the same. I had plans of my own, however.

"Your translator is a liar, and you all need to chill," I blurted out as I shot the translator the deadliest look I could manage. I was furious at the way he was trying to humiliate the Iraqi man. "This man is only asking about the military salaries. Ambassador Bremer mentioned it in one of his televised speeches. The old man is saying he does not want to enter the Green Zone. He just wants to know where he should go."

"Who the fuck are you?" the Iraqi translator and one of the American soldiers shouted simultaneously.

"I am an aid worker," I said as I displayed my badge. "I also speak fluent Arabic. The old man meant no harm. I can't exactly say he is going to leave that way."

"Ma'am, we don't need a smartass in this heat," said the soldier who had been searching through my bag. I noticed Yusuf was also shooting me a deathly stare.

But the soldier lowered his rifle.

"We get the picture," he said. He smiled at the old man and put his hand to his chest, a gesture of apology. I resisted the urge to take off my shoe and beat the Iraqi translator, who now skulked into the background.

The soldiers waved me through, and I stormed across to the convention center. I had a scheduled meeting with Anne Murphy and Kalthoum, but I was so angry that I headed straight for Ivana's desk. This had not been the first translation fiasco I had witnessed, and I wanted to make an official complaint. I knew it would be futile, but at least it would be in some file that historians a hundred years from now might review when trying to figure out how the fabulous plan of winning the hearts and minds of the Iraqi people had gone off the tracks.

Yusuf followed behind me, and I could see that he was fighting back an urge to say something.

"What?" I dared him. "Am I supposed to stay quiet as that idiot did all he could do to escalate the situation? The poor old man had no idea what was happening."

"Manal, you just don't get it. Yes, the translator is an idiot. Yes, he was on some power trip and looking for some drama. But the translators for the Americans are powerful. They are making a lot of money, and I am not talking about their salary. You embarrassed him in front of the soldiers. He will hold a grudge. If he memorized your face, or worse your name, you can bet he will come after you. You have so many enemies just by the nature of your work, do you really want to go out of your way to make new ones?"

He was right. But I also knew that if the cosmos were to rewind time, I would do the exact same thing again.

I felt much more relaxed after seeing Ivana. She walked with me to the room where the civil affairs unit had their main offices, and she introduced me to someone in charge. I was able to vent all my frustrations, and I tried my best not to sound like a school teacher as I explained that the Iraqis who were coming to the Green Zone were not the enemies. However, the humiliation they received just to get some basic questions answered might turn them into enemies, I warned. The soldier kindly listened to me, explaining that the biggest challenge for the U.S. Army was balancing security with the need to do more outreach to the local population.

When I walked out the room, I saw Yusuf sitting with a bunch of Iraqi translators and smoking a cigarette. He stood up when I walked out and all but rolled his eyes when he asked, "*Irtahatee?* (Feel better?)"

I knew he was being sarcastic, but I nodded emphatically. I did. Maybe I was delusional in believing my words would have any impact, but I was happy. At least I had remained true to myself by taking action.

I also remembered the real reason for my being here. Kalthoum.

* * *

As soon as I thought of Kalthoum, I realized how much I was dreading seeing her. We had hit a stone wall in trying to help her. Ironically, this time it was not for lack of solutions. It was just that none were acceptable to Kalthoum. She wanted to go back to her father.

Perhaps it was the fact that the drugs had worn off. Perhaps it was the pregnancy. I secretly believed her twenty minutes at the orphanage for disabled children had shocked her into the reality of her situation. For whatever reasons, we stood at a crossroads.

I called several Iraqi women's organizations for information, as I knew they would be the only people to tell me the truth about her situation. They all confirmed my worse fears: her return to her family would be a death sentence.

Yet Kalthoum was fully aware of this. In her heart of hearts, she seemed to believe it to be a reasonable sentence. Over the span of a few days Kalthoum had developed a strong sense of the cosmic powers of karma, and she begged me to allow her to pay her dues to her family so that her suffering would end.

She explained to me repeatedly that her life was over and that the decisions she had made had left little room for her to start over. However, she had four unmarried sisters at home. Her scandal had reached the tribe. Before, she believed that people would think she had been kidnapped or killed, and there would be no way to confirm she had abandoned her husband and broken the family honor. Now it was confirmed. If she were to go back to her family and face her sentence, then honor would be restored. If she were to run away, then her four unmarried sisters would pay the price. They would be shunned by society and would never marry because of their sister's tarnished reputation. Worse yet, she argued, they would be forced into unsuitable marriages as a third or fourth wife. Her mistakes were hers alone, and Kalthoum wanted to be able to face them directly. She smiled at me and explained that she had been given choices in her life, and she had made the wrong ones. Now it was time for her to pay for her poor choices.

Kalthoum was only sixteen. That was the lone thought that went through my mind as she pleaded with me to help her get back to her family. What life was this girl talking about? What choices? Was she really given a choice when she was married off? Or tricked into prostitution? Was her family really given a choice, fighting to survive war after war and a decade of international sanctions?

I shook my head. I knew that the final decision would rest in my hands. For God's sake, how was I supposed to make such a judgment call? Whatever I would decide would mean life or death for Kalthoum and a string of unpredictable consequences for her sisters. Only in a war zone would a twenty-eight-year-old have so much power.

Fortunately, I didn't have to make this choice myself. I had met a strong Kurdish woman in a conference I had helped plan with Women Waging Peace, an organization formed by former U. S. Ambassador Swanee Hunt. She had established one of the first Iraqi women's shelters to house women from across the country. There were several women's shelters in the northern Kurdish region, but the Asuda organization was the first to accept Arab women. It was also one of the only shelters I knew that would take "untouchable" cases. Untouchable cases were almost always cases dealing with family honor. Asuda would openly help young teenage girls who had been caught having premarital sex, rape victims, and women accused of adultery. Not only did Asuda offer protection to these women, but it also had an entire department dedicated to research and documentation.

Beyond the Asuda organization, I was captivated by Khanim Latif, the woman who led it. I loved her from the first moment I met her. Her fiery eggplant-colored hair with burgundy highlights made her stand out in a crowd. Khanim was a woman ahead of her time. She believed firmly in women's rights and fought passionately for the advancement and protection of women. When I met with her, she was ready to challenge the country's religious and cultural stereotypes. Her warm personality and strong convictions made her a strategic advocate. She had built alliances with key figures in the Kurdish regional government, the *peshmarga* (Kurdish police), and the hospitals. These allies not only helped solve cases but also were instrumental in the documentation process.

Khanim's office was stacked with photo albums of abused women. Her contacts would often tip her off when they received such cases. Khanim would rush over with her camera to take photos, being careful to do so in a way that would protect the women's identity. Entire albums were dedicated to corpses of women. When high-level government officials denied the practice of honor crimes, she would pull out numerous photos of women burned alive or with gun shot wounds and silence her opposition immediately.

After she had turned down suitor after suitor, Khanim decided to never marry in order to dedicate her life to her work. Our friendship was instantaneous, and I developed a dependency on her for thoughtful advice and consultations. I knew she would not shy away from Kalthoum's case like the other Iraqi women did. I knew she would not give me ambiguous advice or simply lay out the consequences. This was a woman who took control. And I prayed to God she would jump in and take control of this scenario.

Indeed she did. The moment she heard Kalthoum's full story, she explained to me that the decision was neither hers nor mine. The decision rested solely with Kalthoum. As long as I was outlining various solutions, it was for Kalthoum to make the final decision. Khanim explained that Asuda believed that the best solution, where possible, was always reconciliation with the parents. There was always a great risk, but she assured me that in many cases it was successful.

"Honor killings happen," Khanim said. "And they happen more than we would like to admit. However, they often happen because our communities have not learned to mediate around such a sensitive topic. No father wants to kill his daughter. Give him an excuse to maintain his honor in front of his tribe, and he will grab on to it. But our community refuses to facilitate such discussions. At Asuda we do. We use religious and tribal leaders to encourage the parents to find solutions other than slaying their daughters. It does not always work, and the proof is in the residents of my shelter. But shelters and relocation are always the second, least preferable option. We are far away from a time when our community will not need those options, but it does not mean we do not keep trying reconciliation."

Khanim advised me to think of someone who could facilitate the discussion with her father. I could not think of anyone until Yusuf reminded me of Munther.

* * *

Munther was pleased to hear from us and to see that we were seeking reconciliation with Kalthoum's tribe rather than what he referred to as kidnapping. He jumped at the opportunity to help. Kalthoum's only stipulation was that her father help facilitate her divorce from her husband. She was willing to live in her father's home, but she could not bear the idea of going back to her husband. Munther managed to negotiate the terms of her return, successfully arranged her divorce, and had the father sign a statement that

Kalthoum would not be harmed if she were to return. Munther also negotiated an agreement with the tribe that he would be able to visit every three months to confirm that Kalthoum was in good health (or to be more blunt, alive).

During the week that Munther spent negotiating with Kalthoum's tribe, Kalthoum waited in the Green Zone. Now that we had sorted out the details for the reconciliation with her parents, all I needed was a sign-off from a U.S. female colonel who had taken a great risk in helping Kalthoum. She, however, was not happy with the arrangement. She had envisioned something completely different, something along the lines of a *Not Without My Daughter*–style of smuggling the teenager across the border. In her mind she saw one of two things: either I was exaggerating the danger to Kalthoum or Kalthoum was insane for wanting to return to her family. Either way, she wanted to get to the bottom of it before she would agree to release Kalthoum.

Kalthoum and I sat in a lobby adjacent to the civil military offices as we waited for a car to take us to meet with the colonel. She leaned over and asked me when she would be able to go back to her family. I assured her it would be within the next forty-eight hours.

"*Alhamdullah* (thank God)," she said. "I am disgusted to be around such filthy women. I cannot wait to get home."

I turned to look in the direction where Kalthoum was glaring. I had half expected to see U.S. soldiers but instead saw a group of young Iraqi women walking across the lobby. I looked back at Kalthoum and could see that she was sincerely disgusted.

"Look at the way they dress," she said. "It is as if someone spray-painted their pants on. You can see every detail of their body." She shook her head as if she were trying to get rid of the disgusting image.

I was speechless. Was it possible that Kalthoum had forgotten the circumstances that led to her being here? I carefully reminded her that her husband and father were demanding her head for her prostituting herself and for carrying one of her client's bastard children. Maybe she wasn't in the best position to be so judgmental.

"Oh, no. I have made atonement," she responded. "I was tricked. I am no longer one of those women." She pointed toward a group of female Iraqi translators sitting in a corner. "Those women bring shame to all Iraqi women."

Like I said, the Green Zone was a place of fantasies.

Chapter Nine

FERN

THE IRAQI FAMILIES WHO SURROUNDED me were an anchor for my sanity. I needed one. Not only was I facing an emotional assault from my work, but my physical problems were creeping up again. This time my back trouble was severe enough to require surgery, and I had started to spend most of my time working from my home in Hay Al Jammah, the university district, a respectable neighborhood that was well known for its resident professors and other faculty members.

I had my own private space in the form of an attachment to the main house, sort of a small townhouse with a separate entrance, kitchen, living room, and bedroom. As I mentioned previously, the Kurdish family who lived in the main house was part of the extended family of one of my dearest friends from high school. I felt safe knowing that the family was so close by, and thus, technically, I was not a Western woman living alone in the middle of Baghdad.

I had no shortage of company. The family made it well known to the neighborhood that I was a longtime friend of their extended family and not some random Arab American who was renting the space. As a result, I was embraced by the neighbors and often invited to tea and to meals.

The family had two daughters, Hawzan and Avienne. They embodied the Iraqi stereotype of Kurdish beauty. Tall and slender, the girls also had a creamy porcelain complexion and wide almond-shaped eyes. They sported highlights by Carol, a well-known hairdresser of the elite. Hawzan had fiery burgundy-colored highlights in stark contrast to her skin tone. Avienne had a mixture of blond and honey-colored highlights that blended with her fair skin. Hawzan was married and lived a few streets from her family. Avienne was nineteen and attended college; she shared the latest university gossip with me over cooking lessons.

My main connection to normalcy when I traveled was finding a way to cook. Avienne was brilliant in the kitchen, and she schooled me in many traditional Iraqi dishes. Every time I make chicken biryani (a rice-based dish layered with chicken, raisins, potatoes, and green peas), I think of Avienne. She taught me the secret of the combination of spices and how to cook the chicken and rice separately. Every night, she stopped by to check in on me.

At the same time, Yusuf's and Fadi's families had adopted me as a long-lost cousin.

Yusuf's mother sent pots of food for me, and his sister, Maysoon, would send her housekeeper twice a week to clean my home and do my laundry. Between them and Avienne, I lived like a princess.

During this time, Hussein and Maysoon would often visit. Maysoon was a social butterfly, and she was eager to introduce me to her network of Iraqi housewives. At the same time, she was eager to trade in her past ten years as a housewife for a career. We often spent late nights talking on the phone about ways that she could look for work with one of the international organizations.

"I want to be a real human being," Maysoon said. "I want to do something to help my people."

But like most Iraqi women, Maysoon was concerned about working for a local Iraqi company. In most cases, only secretarial positions were available. Women working in these jobs often were exposed daily to sexual harassment.

"I want to be helpful," Maysoon would add as she poured tea. It wasn't always easy to concentrate on her words, because her sense of style dazzled me. Maysoon was well known for dressing impeccably, and she often carefully matched her scarf with her outfit. This one was a flamboyant flowing orange, which coordinated perfectly with her purse and shoes. I focused on the way she draped the scarf around her head. It was clear that she had several pins to keep the scarf in place, yet she managed to make it look effortless.

During these visits, I also came to know Hussein. A true representative of the modern Iraqi man, Hussein amazed me with how supportive he was of Maysoon. He loved the idea of her finding work outside their home. He would often tell me stories of the first time they met. They were college sweethearts, and he had admired her vibrancy and confidence during their freshman year. I could easily see it; those qualities still radiated from her. Like Yusuf, she had a determined aura, and I knew that, with a little support, she would accomplish a lot.

When the director of the Austrian-based organization Women Without Borders asked for assistance to identify a local Iraqi volunteer to conduct a survey on women and youth, I instantly recommended Maysoon.

* * *

The family atmosphere in Baghdad made my travels across the country more bearable. I was resisting my body's efforts to slow me down. Despite the fact that I was still recovering from back surgery, I quickly returned to the work of field visits. I alternated one week in the field and one week working from home to recuperate. Every other week I traveled to nearby governorates in Fadi's Peugeot.

During my trips to the south-central governorates it became clear that I had to meet the woman who was quickly becoming a legend in the world of women's issues in Iraq: Fern Holland. All of the women I interviewed, even in the most remote areas of Hillah, Karbala, and Al-Kut, mentioned Fern and her love for Iraq and especially the women of Iraq. Women who met her explained how they were touched by her compassion and determination. They said that they found comfort in the fact that someone working with the United States was looking out for them. Even those women who complained about Fern would compliment her endlessly, only warning that her approach was too fast for the rural areas.

Later, many people tried to paint Fern, a lawyer by training, as a naive feminist idealist with little cultural sensitivity. That description could not be further from the truth. Many times when I went to meet her in Hillah and Karbala, I would find her sitting on the curb and chatting with the guards. The Iraqis were touched by her humble nature and in awe of her fiery passion.

The first time I met Fern was inside the CPA compound in Hillah. As the petite blonde waltzed up to me, I could not help but think of the Iraqis' nickname for her: Barbie. Indeed, she looked like a small toy whipped up by Mattel. Yet the moment she spoke, all images of Barbie evaporated. Fern spoke with authority and confidence, and she immediately demonstrated that she was a woman who liked to be in control.

She plopped down at the table where I was sitting and asked, "I need someone to cut through all the bullshit. Are you that person?"

She did not wait for an answer but instead launched into a tirade of how the window of opportunities to create a new Iraq was rapidly closing. She argued passionately that the people to pay the price were going to be the women of Iraq.

"Manal, I have met women engineers, lawyers, doctors—absolutely amazing Iraqi women who would put most American women to shame. These women are unbelievably strong. And I am afraid we are setting them up for failure. We are giving them nothing but bricks and fancy equipment."

She spoke rapidly and quickly looked me over. "But you know that better than I," she added under her breath as she continued to outline all the obvious mistakes the CPA, the U.S. Army, and the international organizations were making in their approach in Iraq.

Fern was well aware of the risks she was taking by speaking unequivocally about Iraqi women's rights, but she was desperate to make a difference during her time in Iraq. She believed the legacy the United States could leave behind was through Iraqi women. She was committed to establishing women's centers in the areas in which she worked. Fern explained that she had heard about my initiatives and wanted to team up. She had the funds and she could get access to buildings and equipment for women's centers, but she needed someone to help with the softer side of the projects. She needed someone to create programs that would focus on providing women with the training and skills to manage the centers well.

Other Americans and Iraqis had labeled me a cynic and criticized my analysis of the American intervention in Iraq as harsh. Listening to Fern, I was overwhelmed with a sense of validation as I tried to keep up with her. Everything she said spoke directly to me. Most important, Fern refused to stop after she had listed what was going wrong. She insisted on outlining the next steps and some possible solutions to help bring some programs back on track on Iraq.

I was ecstatic. This was the first American working in Iraq who shared my attitude. She refused to side with those who supported the U.S. invasion or with those who wanted the United States out of Iraq. That is, Fern was openly critical but dedicated to delivering that criticism in a constructive manner. We shared the same spirit of creating a long-term vision for the new Iraq, especially for women.

As passionate as I was, my determination paled in comparison to that of Fern. Initially she had been stationed in Baghdad, but she insisted on being sent to the rural areas of Hillah, Karbala, and Al Diwaniyah. Fern argued that a large percentage of the women in Baghdad were educated and among the elite; the women in the rural areas needed international support. At the same time, she was willing to wage battles with everyone from the local Iraqi imam to the highest levels of the CPA leadership.

* * *

During one trip to Hillah, I spent a day with Fern traveling across the city center, looking for an ideal site for the women's center she hoped to establish. She had narrowed our choices down to four buildings. The first three were in remote areas and, without public transportation, women would have difficulty reaching them. The last one was ideal. The structure was large, and it was situated in the middle of the city. The building was in desperate need of reconstruction, but with the funds available through the CPA, that was the last of Fern's concerns.

I remember standing in the midst of the abandoned building. It was perfect. Too perfect. The cynic in me was screaming that there had to be a catch. Why would such a large building in the city center not already have been claimed by one of the Iraqi government councils? We were in the middle of a mass land grab of public property and buildings, and everyone was applying to the CPA for a piece of the pie. I turned to Yusuf and asked him to ask the guards about the building.

Yusuf came back with a grave expression.

"The building belongs to Muqtada al-Sadr," he said.

The doomsday tone in Yusuf's voice was not what alarmed me. Muqtada al-Sadr's name said it all.

At the time, Muqtada al-Sadr was not well known globally. However, among local Iraqi civil society he was gaining popularity by piggybacking on his father's reputation. His father was the Grand Ayatollah Mohammad Sadeq al-Sadr, who was well respected and revered among the Shia community and who achieved martyrdom status in 1999 when he was killed by Saddam. Many Shia leaders would argue that Grand Ayatollah Muhammad Sadeq al-Sadr had become the face of Shia resistance to the Saddam regime. Thus Muqtada al-Sadr was well positioned among the young Iraqi population who were looking for local leadership, and he was among the very few to speak out openly against the U.S. presence.

When the CPA announced the members of the Interim Governing Council (IGC), Muqtada al-Sadr referred to them as U.S. puppets in his Friday sermon that week, gaining him regional popularity for not being intimidated by the Americans. The month before, he had announced plans for creating his own militia and forming a shadow government. Initially dismissed as a young radical by both the American and Iraqi leadership, he claimed a place on the international stage as the leader of the main opposition to U.S. forces throughout 2004.

After Yusuf's news, I looked over at Fern, who stood at the corner of the main foyer and looked across the building. She was smiling. It had been a long time since I had seen her smile, and I knew she had made her decision. I hated to be the one to break it to her that it was the wrong one.

I walked over and explained to her that the building was not an option because it was already claimed by al-Sadr.

"I know," she said. "I am the one who put in the order for the military to throw his cronies out."

I stared at her in disbelief. "What?" was all I managed to say.

"The U.S. administration has promised centers for women. If I don't push forward with full force, it is not going to happen. The political will is here. It's up to me to do the implementation. If they don't give me what I need, I am prepared to take the issue to the international media and embarrass them," she explained.

"I understand," I said. "But it doesn't mean you have to take this building. If such a powerful local group's eye is on the building, you don't want them as an enemy."

"They were squatting here illegally. I had his guys kicked out. They tried to make a stink, but obviously our military guys are much stronger than they are. That's all people understand here—force."

She paused for a second as she glanced around with approval. "They are more than welcome to make a competing application to request the building, but something tells me we will still get it," she added with a smile.

I shook my head. True, the CPA was calling the shots for now. But for how long? She succeeded in having al-Sadr's men thrown out, but they could just as easily come back. Once the building was renovated, the option would be even more attractive. And the U.S. military wouldn't be around. The only people in the building would be women. It didn't take a genius to figure out who would win the argument about force between women and al-Sadr's militia.

I understood Fern's logic. In fact, I had been under the same temptation myself just a couple of weeks before. I had been offered a large building with an indoor pool in the Karrada district for a women's center. The building was then occupied by the guards of the Kurdistan Democratic Party (KDP). I had fallen in love with the building, and more specifically the pool. However, Yusuf and Mais had urged me to turn it down.

The civil affairs unit of the U.S. Army had been working with Capt. Anne Murphy to identify potential buildings for women's centers in nine districts throughout Baghdad. They were growing extremely frustrated with me because I kept turning down the buildings. Why had I done so? Because almost all the buildings were inhabited by strong political parties. In most cases, these parties had their own unofficial militias. I could not afford to make such enemies. I lived in an Iraqi neighborhood with no security, and I was an easy target.

By refusing building after building, there was a strong risk that the army's civil affairs unit would stop assisting us in our search for a building for the women's center. However, in the long run, I felt that the risk was far better than the alternative of creating powerful local enemies who would never leave.

Could I make Fern see this logic? She turned away from me and started walking across the foyer and glancing around the room. In the midst of all the rubble, Fern had traveled forward in time and could see the final product. She was pleased with what she was imagining.

I had also traveled in time, but my vision was much different. Yet something about Fern silenced me. A part of me knew that her decision had been made, and there was nothing I could do about it. But there was more to it. Her determination and fortitude captured my admiration. It inspired a belief that the outcome could be different. I decided to drop out of my role as the killjoy. I said nothing.

It is a decision I have regretted ever since.

Chapter
Ten

THE NEGOTIATING CHIPS

FERN WAS ON ANOTHER RAMPAGE. It was 2 a.m. and she was still responding to emails. She hardly got any sleep. All night we would exchange emails about what was on the horizon for the fight for the rights of Iraqi women.

Subject: Those Bastards

I sent her a quick reply, "Which ones?"

It was always different. Sometimes the rampage would be directed at the Iraqi patriarchal system, at other times it would be about the Iraqi women themselves, who were becoming more and more fragmented. Most often the target of Fern's anger was the Americans—civilian and military alike. The last email chain had been focused on contractors, a scathing complaint about one of the largest U.S. contracting firms, and she itemized in detail her grievances with the contractor.

She wrote emails in what I imagined would be the same style she prepared for court cases. Her notes of time and date were meticulous, and she repeatedly wrote that she would not let the contractors get away with such action. The corruption Fern was describing was outrageous, and I would always feel my body tense up as I read her list of complaints: Millions of dollars were being spent on reconstructing schools, but in most cases it was quite literally a mere paint job. Millions more were being poured into rebuilding the health infrastructure, but the pharmaceuticals and medical equipment wound up on the black market to be resold at three times the cost.

In my work with the women's centers in Baghdad, I was suffering from the same sense of frustration in trying to work with contractors. The funds for the women's centers primarily came in the form of donations through U.S. government contracts. In other words, we were not getting the cash directly; it was sent to the contractors who then provided their services. These services included the repair and maintenance of old buildings and equipment purchases. The contractors would deliver the equipment to the women's center, but there was often a wide gap between what was delivered and what was stipulated on the invoice. For example, we would be charged for an expensive high-end computer, but we would receive an inexpensive basic computer.

Fern and I often refused to sign off on the deliveries.

It was never easy pushing back on issues of quality. Almost all the Iraqi women's organizations were eagerly signing on every dotted line because they were so happy to receive anything to support their efforts. The fact that Fern and I were pushing back was quickly earning us a reputation as difficult women.

But while we were both taking the same action, our approaches were different. I would try to negotiate with the contractors and walk them through the written invoice and compare it to the delivered products. Many times this negotiating process took weeks. Fern simply lacked the patience or the time to negotiate anything. She would refuse the delivery and instantly write a disapproving email to the contractor's supervisor. She was quickly making enemies within the American camp.

* * *

This time, Fern switched her attention to the Iraqi Governing Council and the CPA's blind support for them on issues related to women.

"Those bastards are trying to introduce a law that would revoke the 1959 personal status laws," Fern emailed. Once more she outlined the issue in painstaking detail.

There was a strong lobbying group inside the U.S.-appointed Interim Governing Council calling for an introduction of religious laws when applying the personal status laws in Iraq. These laws covered everything from the right to education to freedom of movement to inheritances to property rights to marriage and divorce, and child custody.

I replied with one word: Impossible. The Iraqi women would never let that happen. The passage of the 1959 personal status law had been the envy of all women's rights movements in the region. It was a source of great pride. The law ensured that Iraqi women could marry under civil law instead of religious law, made polygamy more difficult, granted mothers custody of their children, and imposed a minimum age for marriage. Iraqi women had gained their rights in these and other crucial areas while other countries were struggling. Iraqi women were voting in the 1980s, for example, while Saudi women were still struggling for recognition. Passage of this landmark law capped decades of struggles by the Iraqi women.

If the personal status laws were interpreted through a religious lens, however, the situation had turned dire. In almost all religious interpretations used in the Middle East, personal status laws placed women at a disadvantage.

Fern responded immediately. Her impatience with my naivety was implicit in the email. She felt strongly that Iraqi women would have no choice, and the Kurds had more important priorities to negotiate, such as regional autonomy and federalism. They would not risk upsetting their conservative Shia allies by taking on the personal status laws. That was an issue most political parties were willing to negotiate.

I believed the women would hold strong.

* * *

My six months on the ground had demonstrated what I had known by instinct. Iraqi women were powerful. Through my relationship with Reema Khalaf, the chairperson of the Independent Nahrain Women's Association, I met regularly with the heads of various organizations. These women were predominately engineers, doctors, lawyers, and professors. They were considered the elite of their communities, and often they had their own informal networks that they were willing to use to strengthen the women in their communities. Some of these women had attained the highest level of decision maker.

At the same time, I was able to communicate with women on the ground. I was traveling in and out of the most ghettoized areas of Iraq, including the marginalized areas of Baghdad. Like most of the world's poor, these communities suffered because they were stereotyped as being infested with drug dealers, pimps, and thugs. In some cases the stereotype was true. In most cases, however, the areas were populated with families that were struggling to make ends meet. In every case, the women bore the brunt of any violence and all the poverty.

The majority of women I worked with were widows and divorcees, and some were just teenagers. Despite their difficult circumstances, these women were determined to carve out a better future. I was amazed at their outspoken nature, their candid list of needs, and their resolution to create change for themselves. In the short span of a few months I watched countless women who had entered my office downtrodden emerge from it full of optimism.

Such was the case of Saadiyah. She had learned of our program through word of mouth. Several women in her neighborhood were already enrolled, and as a widow with six children, she felt she had nothing to lose by visiting our office in Karbala. Saadiyah attended the first few sessions reluctantly. Over time, she became more easily involved in the work of the women's center. Not only was she an active participant in the rights awareness workshops, but she signed up for the carpentry class. Saadiyah introduced an innovative way of earning money through carpentry. Each morning she would go to the fruit and vegetable market and collect empty wooden crates. She would then break the crates and use the wood to refurbish furniture.

The women ranged from the elite to the grassroots, and it was an honor to work with each of them. They particularly embodied for me all that our shared culture could accomplish. It was easy to see why their strength was legendary in the Middle East. They had paved the way for women in the region by being among the first to vote, the first to participate in the judiciary system, and the first to demonstrate their economic power. Women from the rural areas became legendary for devising methods to survive the sanctions of the 1990s. The women I met were proud of their ability to survive, and although they were exhausted, they were willing to continue the struggle for a better future.

Nonetheless, these women were not naive. Regardless of their economic status, they were well aware of their violent patriarchal history. They often spoke of the internal conflicts that led to the execution of the king that ended the monarchy in 1958. That was quickly followed by the coup of Gen. Abdul Karim Kassem and five years later to the Baathist regime and then the overthrow of Gen. Ahmed Hassan al-Bakr by Saddam Hussein in 1979. I heard from women of all socioeconomic backgrounds that Saddam's ascension was the beginning of the end. Although the country enjoyed prosperity on one level, the Saddam regime would also lead to hundreds of executions, the Iran-Iraq War in the 1980s, the invasion of Kuwait, the First Gulf War, thirteen years of sanctions, and the Second Gulf War.

For the past few decades, women in Iraq had been forced into the backdrop of Saddam's theatrics. They were used as props when needed. Saddam's approach on women's issues epitomized his Machiavellian quest for power. On the one hand, Saddam was well known for his promotion of women in the workplace and the education of women. On the other hand, he was quick to use women as a negotiating chip to gain local tribal support. For example, Saddam promoted secular laws, but he was willing to turn a blind eye during the 1990s to honor killings in order to appease the tribes. Under the pretext of fighting prostitution in 2000, Saddam's Fedayeen forces beheaded two hundred women "dissidents" and dumped their heads on their families' doorsteps for public display.

By now, Iraqi women realized they needed to take matters into their own hands. Many argued that for too long power had been left unquestionably in the hands of men. They recognized a void had been created, and many were determined to be part of whatever power structure would step up to fill it. Women were focused on the endgame. They were strategizing ways to leap forward, and they refused to be discouraged by the signs surrounding them.

These signs were plenty. Nine months after the fall of the

regime, the dust from the war was just beginning to settle down. It was clear that women's rights were not going to be defended from the outside. It was the responsibility of the Iraqi women to take action from within. Iraqi politicians and the leaders of the American occupying forces made speeches that promised women's rights, but they took no action beyond offering consolation prizes. The threat to women's legal and social status demanded—and received—a response at all levels, from the grassroots to the ruling elite. When the U.S.-led Coalition Provisional Authority refused to swear in a female judge who had been appointed, citing religious and cultural grounds, she fought for her right to the judgeship by using Islamic teachings as her weapon.

Women took these setbacks in stride and still had confidence that their interests rested with the CPA. That is, until Fern's prediction turned into reality.

* * *

On December 29, 2003, with less than a thirty-minute debate, the Interim Governing Council (IGC) voted for Resolution 137. The primary advocate for Resolution 137 was Abdel Aziz Hakim, the leader of the Supreme Council for Islamic Revolution in Iraq (SCIRI). The council was an important political player, and many other political parties that supported women's issues did not want to lose the SCIRI as an ally.

Fern and other women's rights activists around the country went into a frenzy. Resolution 137 would push women's rights back centuries. Whereas Iraqi women had been looking for ways to leap forward, they now found themselves in the unenviable position of fighting for the status quo.

Iraqi women united against the resolution and even took to the streets in one of the first public protests in over thirty years in the streets of Baghdad. These women were among the first members of civil society to immediately practice democratic and transparent management, and they quickly formed the Iraqi Women's Network to fight the resolution. They elected a steering committee, and the network swiftly organized protests and petitions against the repeal of the 1959 personal status laws.

Fern and other international women's rights activists held the U.S. government responsible. They claimed that the IGC was an extension of the Coalition Provisional Authority in Iraq since the IGC had been appointed by the United States. As a result, if the resolution were passed into law, it would be an infringement of international law as defined by the 1907 Hague Regulations. The Hague Regulations forbade any changes to the civil law by an occupying power. Under the Hague Conventions, the IGC's mandate was only to restore public order and safety.

Fern made good on her promise of taking the issue to the public media. She worked closely with Iraqi women leaders to send out reports of the U.S. government's supporting the decay of women's rights, which used terms such as "sexual harassment" and "women's oppression" to get as much attention as possible. She even helped leak an email from a State Department official that referred to Safia Suhail, one of the leading women's rights activists in Iraq, as a loud-mouthed reformist. This email further tied the U.S. government's support and tolerance to the IGC's marginalization of women.

The result of Resolution 137 was far more catastrophic for the women's movement than Fern and the others could have imagined. For the previous six months, women's organizations had been demonstrating the power of cooperation across religious and ethnic divides. I had helped organize a few meetings among women's groups from across the country, and I was always amazed at the mosaic of Iraqi cultures that responded. Secular women shared a round table with their more conservative counterparts; Arabs eagerly expressed interest in learning from the Kurds.

Although all women were united against Resolution 137, the rhetoric of defending women's rights became divisive. International women's groups began to attack core Islamic values. The secular elite from within Iraq joined their voices, and the slogans in the protests could easily be turned into anti-Islamic sentiments. The conservative political parties, such as SCIRI, seized on the opportunity to denounce the protests against Resolution 137 as being orchestrated by Western feminists, therefore reducing the significance of the organic outrage among Iraqi women at this assault on their rights. At the same time, women in the conservative areas believed they were being pushed into a defensive position. They believed firmly in Islamic law, and they were confident that Islamic law was the best vehicle to protect their rights. They instantly jumped to the other side of the spectrum and called for all personal status laws to be rooted in Islamic law. The debate began the division between two extremes: secular versus Islamic law, pro-women versus pro-family.

Women's rights, which had once been a unifying factor, became a source of conflict.

Both extremes were in the minority, and the majority of Iraqi women were torn. When political parties would present the debate as simply choosing Islam over secularism, the vast majority chose Islam. When secularists would outline the rights that would be lost to them, the women grew fearful. Iraqi women wanted to protect their rights, but they did not want to lose their Islamic identity. Most important, as the attacks linking women's humiliation to Islam grew, even the most liberal women felt a powerful, prideful urge to debunk the anti-Islamic myths.

I joined the women in the middle. After all, this was a struggle I had faced my entire life. The balance between my Islamic beliefs and my identity with the Western concepts of democracy and freedom was a trapeze act. For Iraqi women these values were being presented as mutually exclusive. Women were being told they could only make one choice. In the true spirit of the American dream, I wanted it all. I wanted Iraqi women to be able to protect their rights through the rule of law based on the best global practices. I also saw the need for their rights to be defended by using Islamic interpretations to ensure traction on the community level. In other words, what good did it do to have a law that set the marriage age at sixteen when there was no way the government could enforce it? In addition to the law, there needed to be an awareness that demonstrated the need to protect girls from the dangers that early marriage could bring to them and their families.

The problem with Resolution 137 was not simply that Shari'a law was being introduced into personal status matters; the core problem was that there was no attempt to define Shari'a law. Whose interpretations were going to be used? Women would be left vulnerable to the educational limitation and understanding of the local religious clerics. A well-versed religious cleric in Najaf could make a liberal pro-women judgment on inheritance, while a cleric in Basra would deny any women any rights. Without an agreement on the system to be implemented, judgments on women's affairs would be completely arbitrary.

The term Shari'a law was being used as if it had a predefined monolithic classification. There was a legitimate fear that this understanding could lead to serious violations of women's rights, such as denial of education, forced early marriage, domestic violence, execution by stoning, and public flogging.

The division over Resolution 137 caused the Iraqi women's rights movement to lose its comparative advantage of having a wide membership base. Whereas the first few months of the occupation had required only a distinction between Baathist and non-Baathist, finger wagging over sectarian and ethnic divides was now becoming finger wagging over religious and ethnic divides. She is a Shia. She is a Sunni. She is a Kurd. These phrases were becoming more and more frequent and often took on a derogatory tone.

In some instances, the divide centered on attire. Women would quickly label one another based on how much or how little the other wore. A woman who was covered from head to toe would be dismissed as a backward puppet of the Shia conservatives, whereas women who were uncovered were seen as pawns of the Western feminists.

Over time, one's clothing began to play an even greater role. The magnificence of Iraqi civil society in the early months had been the coexistence of women from different backgrounds, each dressed in a unique way to symbolize her individual comfort level. Now the same women who, a few months earlier, had been sitting next to one another and debating everything from integrating women into the political system to revamping the curriculum in the primary schools were openly attacking one another. It only made it more and more difficult for women to identify their true allies.

One of the strongest Iraqi women to emerge in this charged political scene was Salama Al-Khafaji. She wore the traditional black abaya. With the trend of labeling based on physical appearance, her appointment to the IGC received a strong backlash and protests by leading Iraqi women's groups. Over time, however, Salama proved to be an independent woman who was ready to make her own sacrifices for the new Iraq. This would later include the life of her seventeen-year-old son, who was killed during an assassination attempt on her life.

I felt that the debate over Islamic and secular values greatly minimized the larger danger of the resolution. The issue was being minimized as a women's issue alone, but it struck at the very fabric of the newly emerging civil society in Iraq. I would often reiterate to U.S. officials that women should be used as a barometer of success inside Iraq. The status of women highlighted the progress, or lack thereof, of Iraqi society on several levels. Nothing better exemplified this than Resolution 137. In the early months on the ground, any talk of Iraq's becoming another Islamic state, such as Saudi Arabia or Iran, had been dismissed by political analysts and local Iraqis alike. Iraq's history boasted a strong secular legacy, with the understanding that religion belonged in the home, not in the public sphere, and particularly not in the political sphere.

Resolution 137 strongly challenged that assumption.

At the same time, the introduction of the resolution in December 2003 highlighted the beginnings of rising tensions between the ethnic and sectarian divides. The impact on the women's movement was a microcosm of the larger impact on the country as a whole. The introduction of laws being interpreted by each sect foreshadowed the future divides between Iraqi nationals. The 1959 personal status laws had been rooted in secular law, but this whole situation foreshadowed an internal struggle for the entire country. It was the first introduction of formal sectarianism as the foundational base of social and political life in Iraq.

In the end, Resolution 137 was repealed. But over subsequent years it would reappear in new forms, making it clear that Iraqi women had won only a minor battle. The war was yet to begin.

Chapter
Eleven

THE WHISTLE-BLOWER

I CELEBRATED THE NEW YEAR in Baghdad by looking for a doghouse.
During one of my random altercations at a checkpoint outside
the Green Zone, a U.S. soldier questioned me about my living arrangements. When he discovered that I lived in the "Red Zone" (which was
pretty much all of Iraq except for the four square miles that made up
the Green Zone), he immediately launched into a long speech about
personal safety. I told him that no mortar rounds had fallen over my
house in the last week. Could he say the same for the Green Zone?

He laughed and agreed that the Green Zone was not the safest
place to stay either. There had already been two attacks on the Al
Rasheed Hotel, and mortar attacks had become an evening ritual.

Still, his words had some truth. I was now one of the only U.S.
civilians living without armed protection in an Iraqi neighborhood.
A guard dog couldn't hurt.

Attitudes in 2004 were shifting dramatically. For the first six months, the coalition force was convinced that the insurgency would end with the capture of Saddam Hussein. Saddam had been caught in December 2003, but the insurgency continued. Frustration that this prophecy went unfulfilled was reflected in the attitudes of the soldiers. In 2003, U.S. soldiers were thrilled to see the Iraqi civilians. They would joke with me about the fusion of my perfect English and my "local" dress code. They would ask me about Iraqi cuisine and beg me to bring them kebabs.

I found my attitude toward the soldiers melting. These were good guys. Over time I began to recognize most of them at the various checkpoints, and they always remembered me. They would offer me security tips, and each time I was struck by how young they were. More important, though, was how eager they were to learn and understand the country in which they were now living. As we all moved into 2004, this attitude shifted. The soldiers who had entered as an army of liberation rotated out, and a new wave of even younger soldiers, spotted with acne, rotated in.

The locals did not greet these soldiers with roses and tea. Instead, they bombarded them with questions about electricity, water, and employment. These soldiers were frightened and became infamous for being trigger-happy kids ready to raise their weapons at the slightest noise. They eyed me with suspicion every time I ventured into the Green Zone, and they looked at all Iraqis with disdain. This was a manifestation of the bigger picture: the transformation of the U.S. Army from liberators to occupiers in the eyes of the Iraqi people.

A friend who worked in the Green Zone was escorting me in and overheard my conversation with the soldier about getting a dog. The next day she arranged for a tour of the Iraqi zoo, which was still closed to the public.

Dogs are extremely unpopular in most of the Arab world. Iraqi children would abuse any stray dogs they found roaming the streets, so the soldiers would collect stray dogs and shelter them at the zoo.

Although this sounded promising to me, the zoo—home to Uday's lioness and Dobermans—was poorly maintained. The rumor in the streets was that his pets were starving. Iraqis whispered that they had been fed only human meat from his latest victims, and the animals now rejected all food offered them by the U.S. military.

But the animals didn't look like they were starving to me. In fact, they looked full of energy and menace. When I came near their area, they unleashed a stream of howls that made my skin crawl. I quickly moved toward the smaller animals.

The soldiers brought me to a line of cages filled with dogs of different shapes and sizes. There were several puppies, pure-bred German shepherds, and even a couple of Dobermans. As hard as I tried to picture it, though, I couldn't imagine owning one of those as a pet.

Instead, a small dog in the back corner caught my eye. She was the only dog who was not barking and howling. She stood in the corner poised and silent. I instantly fell in love with her. She was cream-colored with brown spots, and she had the deepest brown eyes. I pointed at her and told the soldier that was the dog I wanted. He snorted and made some snide comment about my choosing the worse guard dog ever. I didn't hear him, because the little puppy was already nestled in my arms.

I was lost to the world.

I named her Ishta, which means "clotted cream" in Arabic. I also liked the fact that the word is Egyptian slang for "awesome."

With Ishta in hand, I set about looking for a doghouse. There was something incredibly relaxing in searching for something normal in the midst of chaos. I felt as if I was finally settling in.

* * *

Work was flourishing. We had managed to recruit more than five hundred participants in Baghdad, Hillah, and Karbala, and our job skills training program had launched effectively. In addition to offering training in the more conservative jobs of carpet weaving and hairdressing, we introduced an untraditional course on carpentry, which Saadiyah used so successfully. She was not the only one. Due to the large number of widows and divorcees who were not allowed to call a male carpenter into their homes, a niche existed for female carpenters.

Our office in Shawaka behind Haifa Street had opened in September 2003, and we had finally hired some female staff to work with Muna. The women who joined the team were powerful and enthusiastic. They were dedicated to maximizing every opportunity to make Iraq a better place for women. I recruited women from the areas in which we planned to work, and I made a conscious effort to not limit myself to only elite and professional women. In fact, over the next couple of years, the women who would rise to the challenge of helping the most vulnerable and marginalized Iraqi women came from the most disadvantaged areas of Baghdad. These women navigated the streets of Sadr City, Huriyah, and Shaalah with confidence because these were their own communities.

The female trainers were truly inspiration, and this was clearly reflected in the strength and solidarity of the women who participated in our programs. In addition to job skills training, women came together bimonthly for rights awareness training. After six months the results were awe-inspiring. Several women who had pulled their daughters out of school during the era of sanctions were now reenrolling them.

What's more, the bond between the women in the group was moving. During a session, a new member complained that her family could not afford fruit. She lamented that she had not tasted watermelon in over a decade. One of the women from Shawaka who was among the first to join our program had used the funds she received from the program to start a roadside fruit kiosk. At the next meeting she brought a watermelon to share with the group.

I saw the greatest transformation occur in Muna. With the salary she was now earning, she was able to rent her own place. She also purchased a new wardrobe and was even wearing lipstick. No longer confined to her in-law's house, Muna was now traveling across three governorates, setting up new programs, and scouting for potential participants in the program.

It was a relief to finally be surrounded by these women. Ironically, over the first six months I spent working on women's issues in Iraq, I had been fully dependent on men. First, there was the male staff at Women for Women International. Yusuf, Fadi, and Mais had become my lifelines. I was dependent on them for everything from food and water to the ability to move around the country freely. Within months it became clear that any success I had in launching a program would be directly tied to them. Only years later did I fully grasp the extent of their loyalty; the risks they took were the sole reason I was able to leave Iraq alive. Mark had left the country months before, and my three amigos were by my side from sunrise to sunset and beyond.

Second, there were the male leaders in the communities. From Diyala to Karbala to Tikrit, the one thing that remained consistent across the communities I visited was the need to go through the male elders before ever meeting with a woman. During my trips around the country I would have to meet with a room full of men in order to describe in detail the organization's background and history and to outline the programs we planned to set up for the women of their community. I would then field all kinds of questions from the men. The majority of their questions were almost always personal. Was I married? Why not? Where was my father? What was my background? I never had the option not to answer these personal questions. For the Iraqi tribes, the line between professional and personal was extremely fine. If I were to be granted access to the community, more specifically to the women, they wanted reassurances that I was a person of good moral character.

In almost all the cities I visited I had remarkably similar conversations. After I answered numerous personal questions, their focus would shift to the work of the program, using my background as the first step in addressing their greatest concerns.

"Sister, you are from a Muslim background. You understand what we mean when we say our women are not Western women," was the polite version of the transition in our dialogue from my personal background to the details of the Women for Women program.

In some of the tribal areas, the questioning was more direct. Their primary concern was, "How do we know you are not a Western agent sent to brainwash our women?"

In both cases my answer was the same. All my views on women's rights were deeply rooted in the Islamic tradition. I would explain how I strongly believed the message of Islam was one that preached social justice and change. I felt it was my duty as a Muslim to work with women in conflict to help in their personal struggle from victim to survivor to active citizen. I would casually remind them that the prophet Mohammed (peace be upon him) had been clear in his last sermon that women were important assets to the community. I referred to the many verses in the Koran that emphasize the equality between men and women. I would explain to them how I was proud of an Islamic tradition that had a strong history of powerful women. I would joke about boasting to my American colleagues that the message of Islam was to spread thanks to the influence and wealth of a woman—Sayyidatina Khadija—the Prophet's (peace be upon him) wife.

In almost every instance the men demonstrated a visible reassurance at hearing that Islam was my reference point for working on women's rights. In some of the more religiously conservative areas—such as the Sadrists or the western tribes—the men gave me more details about how women were exalted in Islam.

"Did you know a woman has the right to charge her husband for breast-feeding?" an elderly man from Huriyah explained to me. He told me how this was an example of Islam acknowledging the mother's role in contributing to society's growth. It was also one of the many ways Islam supported the economic independence of women. He further explained that any property a woman acquired by her own work or through an inheritance belonged to her independently of her husband.

A son of a tribal leader in Fallujah outlined for me the women in the historical narrative of Islam. Among the stories he shared was that of Umm 'Umara, a woman who lived at the time of the Prophet (peace be upon him) and fought in many battles. He explained that she was famous for her effectiveness with weapons, and the Prophet (peace be upon him) stated she was better than most men.

I pointed out what I hoped was obvious: somewhere along the line we lost that remarkable tradition, and women had suffered the consequences.

In most cases the conversation was enough to grant me permission to meet with the women in the communities.

In a few cases, however, my Islamic argument was not enough. Their primary fear was that I, as a representative of a Western organization, would poison the women against the men and foment conflict in their communities. The men argued that as long as there were men in the extended families of women, they would be well cared for.

In such cases, I resorted to a wild-card strategy centered on one question: how many adult women live in your household? The majority of families in the impoverished areas had a number of widows, divorcees, and unmarried women under one roof. The

Iran-Iraq War (1980–88) had been dubbed the Spinsters' War because of the large number of unwed women left behind by the vast numbers of men sent to the front line. Worst of all, so many women were left in limbo, because their husbands had gone missing. In some cases they were assumed to be prisoners of war in Iran, but most had disappeared in the middle of the night during one of the many Baathist raids.

Whenever I posed the question to the men about the number of women under their roof, the average answer was usually three adult women and their children in addition to the man's own family. It was not uncommon for the number of women to be twice that many. I would point out diplomatically that these women were an added burden to his household and that his limited resources were being stretched thin. An essential part of the Women for Women program was teaching job skills to women to allow them to generate their own income. I subtly insinuated that this additional income would not only empower the women in my program but significantly ease the burden on the male heads of household who were struggling to feed their own children.

The third way in which I was dependent on men involved my finding someone within a community to make the introduction for me to the community leaders. I could not suddenly appear at a city center and announce that I was there to discuss women's programs and debate women's roles with in Islam. Someone known and accepted in the community had to facilitate my presentation. This process allowed me to enter the areas of Karbala and Najaf successfully as early as August 2003.

* * *

At some point during my first few months in Iraq, I came across Ashraf Al-Khalidi, a young civil society activist. His sense of dedication toward the new Iraq bordered on obsession. He was a handsome Iraqi professional who took advantage of every opportunity to broadcast the great ideals the United States had brought to Iraq. It quickly became apparent that this was more than mere lip service for him. He believed in those ideals, he was committed to them, and he was ready to sacrifice his life to see them take root in Iraq.

Many years later the U.S. government recognized Ashraf as one of the Iraqis who took a great personal risk by aligning himself with America. The government granted him a special immigration visa, but Ashraf refused it. His sacrifices had never been for the Americans; they had been for Iraq.

Ashraf saw the potential in a democratic Iraq, and he worked day and night to fulfill his role in making it happen. He was a native of Karbala, and he urged me to expand my programs into the governorate.

As a single woman traveling the country alone, I had few options for places to stay. Since my objective was to meet with tribal and community leaders, the option of staying at a local hotel was ruled out instantly. Why? It was strongly believed that only a certain kind of woman would stay at a hotel alone. For the same reason, I ruled out the option of staying at the CPA or at a military base. My impartiality was my main entry point into some of the most conservative areas in the country, and I could not afford to compromise that for accommodations. In such cases I would stay at the homes of extended families of Iraqi friends and staff. This had the added benefit of providing me an opportunity to fully grasp the daily life of Iraqis.

Among the most memorable homes was that of Ashraf's family. Although he was based in Baghdad, his family home was in Karbala's city center. Ashraf had six sisters; two were married and four were still at the family home. His father had passed away and, as the oldest son, Ashraf was considered the head of the household.

Despite his living in Baghdad, he still called the shots back home. The fact that Ashraf was an active member of civil society strongly distinguished him from other male heads of households. He urged his sisters to continue their education and encouraged them not to rush into marriage. I was touched at the way his sisters would run to greet him, love and admiration radiating as they embraced him each time he visited.

The moment Ashraf and I would arrive from Baghdad, a large feast was prepared, and the girls would hurry a round the house to prepare the meal. Once we had eaten, the family spent hours catching up on everything from the latest soap operas to current affairs. At night, mattresses would be pulled into the main living room, where all the women would sleep. It was a large house with plenty of rooms but no electricity. A small generator had been purchased, but it operated only a couple of fans.

Electricity problems were not uncommon. Every community-needs assessment conducted by humanitarian organizations indicated that electricity was the number-one community priority. Years later, several military strategists attributed the failure to restore electricity in Iraq as one of the CPA's key failures in establishing security in Iraq. From the beginning, however, the insurgents knew this. Energy plants, power lines, and neighborhood generators were targeted weekly. Their goal was to undermine the CPA and Iraqi government officials, and their plan worked well. Many Iraqis lost confidence in the United States as a result of the unreliability of utilities. Women complained they could not access water (because pumps operated on electricity), their children studied by candle light, and their infants cried all night due to the suffocating heat. Previously simple tasks such as laundry turned into strenuous chores.

It was one thing to hear the complaints; it was another to live it. During those nights without electricity my body fought between exhaustion and the oppressive heat that refused to let me sleep. Some women dipped towels in cold water and wrapped them around their hands and feet before they went to sleep. I often lay in silence all night and prayed exhaustion would take over and force my body to sleep. Instead I would toss and turn in a semiconscious state, suspended between the desire to sleep and the sounds of whistles blowing throughout the night.

As a result of the vacuum in local security that began in 2003, the men in Karbala had developed a neighborhood watch system to maintain law and order in their communities. A member of the neighborhood watch monitored each street corner, and they would blow whistles every five minutes to indicate all was well. This was long before the debate on Iraqis taking responsibility for their own security. The men of Karbala instinctively knew that they would have to tend to their own safety measures if they wanted to keep their families safe.

Instead of counting sheep, I counted the moments until the next whistle. Just as I approached three hundred, I would hear a whistle and start counting over again.

Chapter Twelve

PLAYING WITH FIRE

WHEN LIEUTENANT MCBRIDE—I NEVER knew her first name—opened the door to the trailer, I saw five Iraqi girls seated on bunk beds: two on the top mattress, three on the bottom. When they saw me, the three on the bottom made a futile effort to scramble toward a hiding place in the narrow trailer. The two on top buried their faces in the bed's thin pillows.

I stared in disbelief. With their fake green and blue contact lenses, badly highlighted hair that had taken on an orange hue, and tight-fitting, crystal-studded jeans with tight tank tops, they looked neither Iraqi nor American, but rather like some sort of misconstrued hybrid. I knew right away that I was in over my head by agreeing to meet with them. Five girls from Baqubah living inside an American trailer in the Green Zone spelled trouble.

During our walk from the palace being used as U.S. military headquarters to the trailers, McBride told me that the girls—five cousins who had run away from home—had entered the Green Zone only after they had been promised they wouldn't have to interact with any Arabs. Still, their initial reaction to me caught me off guard.

"Ya prohmise me," the oldest of the girls—the ringleader, no doubt—shouted out in broken English. Of the five, she had the brightest orange highlights. Her fiery hair, combined with her eerie blue contact lenses, gave her a demonic appearance.

"She's an American," responded McBride with reassuring confidence. When the lieutenant had initially seen my head scarf, she, too, had been worried. The girls had convinced her that Arab women would not sympathize with their plight. But during our walk from the palace to the trailer, I told the lieutenant about some of the cases I had handled in the last six months: rape victims, prostitutes, and victims of honor crimes. McBride seemed to relax with each step we took. I wasn't sure if it was because of my experience in dealing with women in difficult circumstances or my crisp American accent.

"Yes, I'm an American." I told the girls. "And I work for an international women's organization. I've helped many girls like you, and trust me, the things I've seen can't be any worse than what you're about to tell me."

I spoke softly in English to quell any fears about my Arab origin, even though I knew speaking in Arabic would have been easier for them to understand.

I leaned against the trailer door, trying to look as casual and nonthreatening as possible, and the lieutenant stayed outside and just behind me. The sky had already begun to break out into sunset shades of red and orange. As soon as darkness fell, the temperature would drop. The chill of January nights in Baghdad was almost as torturous as the heat of July days. I wished I hadn't left my coat in Lieutenant McBride's car. Still, no matter how cold it was, I did not want to enter the girl's tiny space unless they invited me in.

One of the girls on the top bunk lifted her face from her pillow and looked down at me. She didn't look a day over ten years old, although later I learned that she was twelve. Her waist-long hair was twisted into an impromptu braid that she kept twirling over her shoulder. With her head tilted slightly, she asked, "If you're an American, why are you covered?"

"I am a Muslim. I cover because I have chosen to. The important word is *chosen*." I was surprised by my non sequitur, but instinctively I knew that I needed to keep talking. It didn't matter what I said as long as I said it in English. It was clearly working.

One of the girls, who had convinced herself that she was invisible behind one of the thin bed posts, peeked out at me and asked in a timid voice, "Are your parents Iraqi?"

"No," I replied. "I have only been here a few months."

"You came with the Americans?"

"No, not at all. I'm here with humanitarian aid workers. My job is to help women. I have nothing to do with the military."

The ringleader sat down on the bottom mattress and stared at me defiantly with eerie eyes. "We only talk army people. Only U.S. soldier we trust. We give information, and now they take us to America."

I later learned that her name was Zeena. She was sixteen, and she had masterminded the girls' little adventure.

"That's fair," I replied calmly. I knew it was important that they understand what I was about to tell them, but I also worried about switching from English to Arabic, consciously thickening it with what my close friends call my Texas Arabic accent.

"Look, the soldiers can't do anything for you except keep you in this trailer. And even that they can only do for no more than a month. They called me because they know I may be your only chance. We need to figure out a more realistic solution for you, and I can help them do that. But only if you want me to."

"We no want your help," Zeena snapped back, speaking loudly in English for the sake of the lieutenant, who apparently knew only five Arabic words.

"Okay," I said, still standing outside the trailer. I shrugged my shoulders and started to withdraw, closing the door behind me.

"Wait," said the girl sitting next to Zeena. She turned to Zeena and said very sharply in Arabic, "We have been here three days, and I cannot keep sleeping in this trailer. The food is horrible, and we need to know what the hell is going to happen to us. Maybe she can help. Let's at least talk to her."

I remained silent, the trailer door slightly ajar. Now all five faces looked at me. This other girl was close to Zeena's age. Her name was Rasha. The remaining three girls were clearly very young and very scared. I wanted to pull the young ones to me and give them a long, tight hug. What horrible thing had happened to them to force them into this situation?

Not waiting for Zeena or Rasha to come to an agreement, the youngest on the top bunk blurted out, "We ran away from home. There is no way we can go back. We thought the military would send us to America, but now we do not know what to think." She was close to tears.

"*Inchaabi*! (Shut up!)" Zeena screamed, standing up and whirling herself around to face the little one.

"You do not need to tell me anything now," I said, trying to defuse the situation. I opened the door and placed one foot inside the trailer. Zeena's fierceness made me afraid to leave the little ones with her. "Instead, why don't you ask me questions and get to know me. If you feel there is something I can do for you, then fine. I will be happy to come back tomorrow. If you don't, then you never have to see me again, and I will forget I ever met you. Deal?"

Zeena did not answer. She just sat back down and didn't interrupt when the rest of the girls started asking me questions. I sat at the edge of the entrance to the trailer, leaning my back against the open door. My feet dangled freely outside, and I crossed my arms for warmth. For the next fifteen minutes we talked. They asked about my job and seemed impressed to hear that I traveled so extensively. They were thrilled to hear I had been to Kenya and Afghanistan, and even Zeena seemed to open up by sharing that her dream had always been to travel all over the world. The younger girls—Zahra, Iman, and Amani—formally introduced themselves. Amani, the youngest, was only nine. Both Zahra and Iman were twelve years old.

I found myself enjoying talking to the girls and even managed to forget how cold I was. By the time a colonel came by to check on us, the tension had dissipated, and the girls were shooting questions at me.

The colonel stood to the side and cleared his throat. Taking my cue from him, I stood up. "I have to go now. I do not know if I will see you again, but I will be thinking of all of you. I know you girls are smart and brave, so I will not worry about you too much."

With that, Lieutenant McBride and I made our way back to the palace, and I waited for her in the parking lot to get her keys to the Toyota Land Cruiser. I was already frozen to the core, so another five minutes outside wasn't going to kill me. She would have to drive me back to the convention center, where my driver was waiting.

As I waited, I realized I had broken my promise to myself not to get involved when the U.S. Army randomly intervened in the lives of Iraqi civilians, especially women. The stubborn bull in me simply refused to learn her lesson. My staff was still frustrated by the last incident: the army contacted us when a soldier's chivalry led to the arrest of a man who had allegedly threatened his wife at a vegetable stand in Baghdad. When the man was released three days later, he threw his wife out of the house and divorced her. When we failed to reconcile the couple, all we could do was enroll the woman in our job skills training program to help her earn an income. What she described as a simple market place squabble ended up leaving her with no protection or livelihood.

Years of humanitarian work had taught me that the smallest intervention could set loose an avalanche of unexpected consequences. I knew better than to dive in on a whim. The key was to anticipate and plan for worst-case scenarios and to take calculated risks to improve people's lives. Even the most experienced aid workers could find themselves stuck in some intractable situation. My organization's motto was "Underpromise and overdeliver."

Somehow, the U.S.-led coalition had overlooked this lesson. Every day the gap between rhetoric and reality grew wider. Well-meaning individuals in the military were so zealous about providing assistance, they made outlandish commitments. As a result, the military was left to handle cases far beyond its jurisdiction. When those cases involved women, they often found their way to me.

Case in point: the five Pandoras who had opened a box without thinking of the consequences. Once again, I'd been dragged into a complicated situation made intractable now that the U.S. military was involved.

Capt. Anne Murphy had called me about the girls' situation. She did not know any details, but a colonel had asked her to put him in touch with an American women's nongovernmental aid organization. At the time of her call, she explained that I was the only person she could recommend with a clear conscience. Her faith in me meant a lot, and I couldn't just turn away. Over the last few months I had begun to look at Anne as more of a friend than a colleague. I agreed to see the girls as a favor to her.

Since Anne's intervention with Kalthoum, we had worked on several projects together. Primarily we were both intent on seeing a women's shelter open in Baghdad to provide a safe haven for marginalized women. We had also begun work on the women's center project. We quickly became inseparable. Becoming friends with a U.S. soldier was the last thing I had expected, but Anne won me over with her dedication and integrity.

She was a native of Boston, reared in a liberal family, and an advocate of what she called hard-core Democratic beliefs. She was one of the only people I knew in Baghdad who had voluntarily enlisted after the war in Afghanistan started. Most of the soldiers I knew had either joined the reserves, an ROTC program in college, or were on a long-term career track in the army.

During one of our first meetings, Anne had described the circumstances that had led her to enlist. From her point of view it was only a matter of time before President Bush and his cronies messed things up. At the same time, she felt she could not just sit back and watch bad things happen. She decided to enlist in order to be at the front lines with her countrymen to try to bring about a positive change.

"Even if it's just changing the lives of the people I meet directly, at least I feel I am doing something," she explained. I liked her immediately.

Besides my personal dedication to Anne, I was really touched by the looks on the faces of the girls as I left the trailer. I sincerely wanted to do my best to help them, but it was clear that Zeena, the oldest, didn't want me to. I didn't know whether to leave Zeena in charge and just walk away or to force my help on them for the sake of the little ones. My rational side told me not to get involved, but my emotional side was already thinking of solutions. Part of me wanted destiny to take control of the situation and for Lieutenant McBride to tell me the girls didn't want my help.

When the lieutenant arrived with her car keys, her cell phone was pinched between her shoulder and her ear. She quickly finished the call and said,. "Well, they want you back. Can you come tomorrow?"

"Sure," I said. I was surprised that instead of dread I felt a sense of relief sweep over me. I wanted to stay involved because I was afraid for the younger girls. Zeena thought she was calling the shots, but she had no idea what she was doing.

And I still had even less insight into what was really happening. Under what circumstances had the five girls run away from their homes? Why would they undertake such a crazy risk? I needed to collect a little intelligence of my own.

Before I went to sleep that night, I decided to call Abdullah, a police sergeant in Baqubah who was always eager to help me. I asked him if he had heard about the disappearance of a group of girls, but I omitted any mention of my meeting with them. He told me he would look into it and get back to me.

* * *

The next morning I woke up early and headed to the Green Zone for my ten o'clock appointment with the girls. Access to this secure area was gradually becoming more difficult. When I had first arrived six months earlier, anyone could walk up to the sidewalk in front of the convention center, which sat in the middle of the Green Zone and served as the main administrative contact point between Iraqi civilians and the Coalition Provisional Authority. There had only been one checkpoint, which was a quarter of a mile from the convention center's main entrance. Now visitors had to walk more than a mile through a corridor of sand bags and barbed wire and pass through three checkpoints. Special badges and body searches were required to get past the first barbed-wire checkpoint that encroached on a busy intersection perpendicular to Haifa Street.

I met Lieutenant McBride in the usual place at the convention center, and we drove to the Republican Palace, which had been turned into the seat of power for the CPA. The drive from the convention center to the palace was still a delight. A year later, the same area was turned into a labyrinth of ugly concrete slabs, razor wire, and bunkers, with checkpoints scattered around like weeds. But in 2003 the gardens were well manicured and three-story-tall bronze busts of Saddam Hussein stood insolently at the four corners of the palace, as if to remind us of where we really were.

We headed straight for the girls' trailer and were surprised to find it empty. Soldiers from the neighboring trailer told us the girls had headed off to the cafeteria.

"Those girls are very high maintenance," McBride said, rolling her eyes. "They've only been here three days. But they've been complaining every hour, minute, and second of the time. Somehow they expected to get the royal suite inside the palace," she added with exasperation. "Don't get me wrong, I have grown to really like them. But they act like they're on some adventure—not like they're seeking asylum."

Now that I had been invited back, I was determined to get more details from them. There was no way I could be of any use if their circumstances remained ambiguous. We walked into the cafeteria. This was only the second time since I had arrived in Baghdad that I had come to the public area of the old palace. The first time I visited, I had been overwhelmed by the gaudiness of the interior design, an opulent hybrid of the Blue Mosque of Istanbul and the Palace of Versailles outside Paris. I was disgusted that Saddam and his belligerent sons might have stood in the very place where I was standing.

This time I was struck more by the juxtaposition of the high school–style cafeteria that spread out across the public area and the walls of the ornate building that rose up around it. At the tops of the walls, high above the dining soldiers' heads, were biblical or Islamic proverbs—falsely attributed to Saddam, of course—carved in elaborate Arabic calligraphy. Above the arched entryway to the former ballroom, now transformed into a canteen, one of the carvings read: "Do not dismiss the simpleton who debases your reputation, for how many pebbles fracture a large glass?"

The clashing mix of Saddam-esque opulence and military austerity was the perfect stage for the five young girls who blended amazingly well into the sea of army uniforms. We found them at the back of the cafeteria, sitting with a group of soldiers. The soldiers were taking turns having their pictures taken with the girls, who were clearly less frightened than the night before. In fact, the older two looked ecstatic.

"Manal! Manal! Come over here!" the youngest, Amani, called to me.

I went to join them and introduced myself to the soldiers. The two older girls were perched at the edge of the table, their feet dangling above the ground. Every few seconds they would giggle for some reason. My initial feeling of discomfort resurfaced. The lieutenant's description of these girls as adventure seekers had been spot-on. I knew that their parents would be furious if they saw their daughters' behavior now. Even in the most liberal societies, the image of these young school girls hanging out among a group of male soldiers would churn stomachs. It was one thing to assist helpless women and girls, but there wasn't any helping going on here.

Every few minutes Zeena's and Rasha's giggles would crescendo into a shriek of laughter. The three younger girls were sitting around the table, beaming at the two older ones. I had to resist a sudden motherly urge to yank them away from the table and scold them. Instead, as nonchalantly as I could, I said hello and asked how they were.

"Good, good," Amani responded. "This morning we took a picture with the famous American. They promised to make copies for us to take home." She was speaking in Arabic and was clearly excited about all the attention the soldiers were giving her.

Zeena and Rasha, still perched on the edge of the table, posed between three soldiers who were leaning in behind them. They all put their hands up and gestured with the peace sign. I wanted to vomit.

The picture taking made me feel like these young girls were trophies to the soldiers. None of the troops seemed the slightest bit concerned that the five girls were stranded with no place to go. They clearly had no idea of the expectations they were setting in these girls' minds—or they simply did not care.

I remembered what Amani had said last night—they had hoped they would be sent to America. I knew there was no chance of that happening. I decided to get to work.

"Listen, girls, I do not have much time this morning. Let's sit on the side so we can have a proper chat." I sounded a bit more frantic than I would have liked.

"Relax," Zeena drawled, dragging out the word and rolling her eyes at me.

I walked over to another table, and Amani and the other girls followed. Zeena stayed behind with the soldiers.

"All right," I said, "tell me what happened. Start from the moment you decided to leave."

Rasha began to tell me the story. The girls' fathers were brothers, and their families lived together in one house in Baqubah. One evening they heard their parents speaking with their older brothers. The brothers were planning an attack on the nearby coalition army base. For two nights Zeena and Rasha could not sleep. According to Rasha, the cousins felt they had a moral obligation to warn the soldiers who had liberated their city from Saddam. That, she said, was why they set out on their journey.

Rasha sounded as if she were reading from a script. When I asked why they didn't go to a nearby post, why they traveled all the way to Baghdad, none of them could answer.

Zeena finally decided to grace us with her presence and quickly took over where the girls had gone silent. She explained that they had been worried that one of their parents' friends or relatives would see them, and so they kept moving until they felt they were at a safe enough distance to approach a base.

"But why take your little sisters?" I asked.

Rasha and Zeena both responded immediately that they could not trust them with their families.

I carefully looked at the five girls. They all seemed to be well cared for. It was clear that the highlights in their hair had been done a while ago. True, it looked more like they had been attacked by kindergartners armed with Sun-In, but not many families in the governorates outside Baghdad could afford to have their daughters' hair highlighted. Or buy them colored contact lenses. The younger girls were chubby, so it was clear they were well fed. Something seemed very wrong.

Their story was not very convincing, but now there was a much bigger problem. Whatever the particular circumstances were around their running away, these girls had now been missing from their homes for about a week. There was a chance of reconciliation if the parents believed they had been taken against their will, but it was slim. The idea of young girls being unaccounted for over several days would raise many questions about the family's honor. Few Iraqi men were willing to take the risk of shaming their family's name. Even if the girls' fathers demanded an examination to ensure that the girls had not been violated, and they passed, there would be enough suspicion about the length of their absence. If the parents had the smallest clue about what really happened, there was no doubt in my mind the girls would be killed. In their parents' opinion, the girls would have committed two terrible crimes: betraying their fathers and spending time away from their families without chaperones. The fact that they had been among Americans would only exacerbate the shame.

It was clear to me that these girls would never be able to go back home.

"So what are you thinking now?" I asked them.

"We came to join the army. We want to enlist," Zeena boldly stated.

"Excuse me?" I was sure I had heard her wrong.

"Yes, we want to fight with the Americans against terrorists. It doesn't make sense for them to fight for us."

I was shocked. This sixteen-year-old girl had lost her mind. "You know that's not possible."

"Why not?" She demanded. "I have seen many young people on television who fight for their country. "

I had no clue what to do with that statement. I wasn't prepared to go into the obvious reasons as to why her logic was ludicrous, so I simply said, "You have to be eighteen to enlist."

Zeena was silent for a second before she burst out, "Then they can send us to America, and when we turn eighteen, we will join the army." She seemed adamant that her plan was foolproof. I realized there was no reasoning with this girl.

I turned to Rasha, who I prayed would be the saner of the two. "I can help you. There is an organization I work with in Sulaymaniyah, in northern Iraq, and they have helped place young girls like you. The situation there is different, and at least we will know you are safe."

"What will we do there?" Rasha asked.

"Stop it! Stop talking to her." Zeena jumped in. I looked over at Amani and the other two, who hadn't said a word so far. They had the same frightened expression I had seen on their faces last night. This only made me angry with Zeena, who was beginning to make the possessed girl in *The Exorcist* look like a girl scout.

"Can't we stay here?" Amani meekly asked.

"I wish you could." I said, deciding to try to stay on their good side. "I am totally with you. Believe me, if I thought you could get to America or even stay here, I wouldn't even get involved. But you can't. That's why they've called me. They don't know what to do with you, and time is running out."

"What will we do if we go to the north? Have you been there?" Rasha asked me, clearly making an attempt not to look at Zeena.

"I've been there. It's a very nice house. I personally know the woman who represents the organization here in Baghdad, and I also know the woman who is in charge of the house in Sulaymaniyah. She's a good friend, and I go there every three months. If you are interested, we can look into it. I would even go with you to Sulaymaniyah, so you wouldn't need to make the trip alone."

Amani and Rasha looked carefully at me. Apparently they were sisters. The other little ones were Zeena's little sisters and would not dare question her. Zeena seemed to calm down a bit, and she leaned forward.

"You are a nice woman," she said. "Maybe one day I would even want to hear more about your life and where you have traveled. But you are ruining everything. Now the only option is for them to send us to America. With you, there will be another option. I will die before I go to the north, and I will kill myself in that nasty trailer they have put us in. So stay out of this. *Iftahamtee?* (Do you understand?)"

* * *

There was not much I could do or say after that. The girls had to ask me for help, and even if I were crazy enough to try to force my help on them, I knew that my partner organization would ask for a signed consent form from the girls. Even though my heart reached out to the younger girls, there was nothing I could do for them as long as they refused to cooperate.

I would have to explain the situation to the colonel.

From my first meeting with the colonel a few days earlier, our interaction had been tense. He knew that I was an Arab American aid worker, but apparently nobody had bothered to mention that I wore a veil, which I could tell he interpreted as a sign of extremism. He gave me a mini-interrogation to confirm my Americanism. What brought me to Iraq? Where was I from? Why did my parents choose to start their lives in the United States in Lubbock, Texas? Why did they move to Spartanburg? Why was I Muslim? I answered all of his questions, no matter how personal or private. He seemed to be comforted by my responses and became a bit friendlier—but only a tiny bit.

I left the girls and went to the building where the colonel's office was located and asked for him at the makeshift security desk that was set up in the foyer. I sat on a bench and waited. When he showed up fifteen minutes later, he didn't bother inviting me into his office.

"You asked for me?" He stared blankly at me.

"Yes, sir," I said, wincing at the sound of the word *sir* coming out of my mouth. "I need to let you know that I will not be able to help you with the girls."

"And why is that?" he asked, a hint of worry creeping into his expression.

"Sir," I said, mad at myself for calling him "sir" again, "I can't get involved if they don't want my help. They told me in very clear terms they do not want our organization, or any other NGO for that matter, involved. Only the military."

"I thought you said there was a shelter in the north. I can arrange transportation and send them there. What's the problem?"

"They don't want to go, sir." *Damn!* "I can only take them if they go voluntarily, and they have to agree to the conditions of staying. They won't."

"It is not up to them—do you understand me?—IT IS NOT UP TO THEM!" He barked each overenunciated word at me.

I weighed my response and calmly replied, "They are all under the age of eighteen. I cannot force them to relocate, either as an individual or as a member of the NGO for which I work. First, they will probably run away again. Second, in most countries that's considered kidnapping."

"They have to go," he said. "Those little punks gave us empty information. We conducted a thorough investigation, and their claims were bogus. Those little brats tricked us! And now they are stuck to us like leeches."

"You guys are treating them like tourists," I said. "Did you ever even talk to them about the consequences of taking them in? For them, this is the adventure of a lifetime. Of course they don't want to go. You don't just take in girls as young as them without telling them what's going to happen to them." There was anger in my voice now.

"That is their problem, not mine," the colonel said. "As far as I'm concerned, the U.S. government has been extremely gracious with them, and I have gone beyond the call of duty. Now you need to do your job and place these girls!"

"Yeah, well you should have thought about that when you decided to keep them on a U.S. military base. It's too late to backtrack now!" I was almost yelling at him. "The fact of the matter is that if their parents discover where they've been for the last few days, they will most likely be killed. You have a responsibility for their lives."

Without hesitation he snapped back, "Either you take them or I'm going to pack them into a Land Cruiser, drive them down to Baqubah, and boot them out into the desert where they came from."

His arrogance was amazing. I thought to myself, *This is not my problem, and I will not get involved.* I kept saying that in my head, trying to convince myself, but it didn't work. I couldn't walk away from these girls and leave them at the army's mercy. This was about the girls, not the colonel. Yes, they had done a very stupid thing, but didn't we all do stupid things without fully realizing the consequences? In the end, this would be about life or death.

I took a deep breath and looked up at the colonel. "I will try again," I said. "They have it stuck in their mind that you can help them and I'm ruining everything. You need to make sure they know they are out of options, so they will take a bit more seriously whatever alternative I provide. In the end, it is not my decision to make. It will be the decision of the women's shelter. The director's name is Khanim. I will arrange for her to come and interview the girls."

"Is she with an Iraqi organization? If she is, she cannot interview the girls. I made a promise they would not have to meet an Iraqi organization."

"It is not up to you," I said a bit abruptly, and then softened my tone. "Khanim is a Kurdish Iraqi, and she is the only one who can accept the girls at this point." I added for extra softness, "Sir."

I was half lying. I knew Khanim would accept them based on my referral, but she would never forgive me if I didn't give her fair warning that these girls were being moved involuntarily. I suspected they might run away as soon as they arrived.

"It's not going to happen. Do you have any other recommendations?" the colonel asked.

"I can have one of my local staff do the intake interview on Khanim's behalf. I cannot do it myself because my Arabic writing skills are not strong enough to write the intake report, and I would not be able to complete the forms needed," I said, thinking of Muna. "But just for the record, I am doing this for the girls, not for you."

"Yeah, well, I don't really give a rat's ass why you're doing this," he said. "Just get them out of here."

* * *

I left the Green Zone furious at the incompetent soldiers who had brought in these girls without giving a second thought to the implications of their actions. I felt particularly angry that it was left for me to clean up the blasted colonel's mess. But I tried to think less about his motives and to focus on the girls themselves.

Yusuf had a serious expression on his face when I returned to the office. "You may want that lip at some point," he said. It took me a second to realize that I was alternating between chewing my lower lip and pulling it back and forth like bubble gum—my trademark tic when I was lost in thought.

He had a message for me from Abdullah, the policeman I had contacted in Baqubah for information on the girls. He had come all the way to Baghdad and needed to see me as soon as possible. Abdullah would come back to the office that afternoon. It was already two o'clock, so I knew that he would probably show up at any minute.

Before he arrived, I decided to update Yusuf on the girls' situation. As I poured out the details, along with a side dish of commentary, I realized how great it was to have someone to confide in, even if it meant getting one of Yusuf's infamous lectures. A typical Yusuf lecture would often begin with: "Manal, the Koran tells us not to throw ourselves in the fire pit, and to take an easy route instead of a difficult one when the choice presents itself. Why are you hell-bent on jumping in, taking a swim, and floating around in the fire pit?"

A lecture was a small price to pay for the assurance of knowing

Yusuf would be by my side. It would have been impossible to tackle such difficult cases without his ability to advise me on the Iraqi context. And he was adept at maneuvering around red tape, both official and informal. Although we often disagreed, I knew I could always trust him. I needed his counsel now more than ever.

Abdullah arrived twenty minutes later. He was middle-aged, about five feet three inches in height, with a muscular frame and perfect posture. Despite his small stature, he spoke and moved with such authority that he instantly filled the room with his presence. People would always gravitate toward him in our community meetings.

But today he arrived looking pale, with a worried look on his face. He slouched in the seat in front of my desk and fidgeted while trying to decide which way to cross his legs. Anxiety started to well up inside me. It wasn't like Abdullah to make the trip to Baghdad unannounced. I was praying that he would tell me he was just dropping in because he was in the neighborhood—but how likely was that when your neighborhood was in Baghdad?

The moment we received our chai, he asked, "How did you know about the boys' case?"

I lowered my tea glass and looked at him. "What boys?"

Abdullah gave me a suspicious look. "The two brothers who were caught two days ago. They have been in interrogation. Even I did not know about them. How did you know?"

"I have no idea what you are talking about, Abdullah. What does this have to do with me?"

Annoyance crept into his voice: "The brothers who are responsible for kidnapping the Al Mitwakal girls?"

I looked at him in horror and disbelief as the dots began to connect. "I had no idea that the girls had been kidnapped," I stuttered, completely confused as to what I could or should reveal. "I just heard there was a possibility of some girls from Baqubah that went missing, and I wanted to see if there was any truth in the rumors."

Abdullah remained silent, perhaps not wanting to believe me, but also not able to dismiss the utter shock on my face. I was beginning to feel physically sick at the realization that two innocent men were being detained for five girls who had voluntarily run away. "How do they know these men kidnapped them?"

"Well, they apparently have confessed."

The sick feeling worsened. What had been done to these men to extract such a confession? "Where are they being held?"

I was already mentally rehearsing my phone call with Captain Murphy, my main ally and the person who had initially called me about the case. She needed to know about this, and given her aversion to torture, I was sure I could persuade her to look into it.

Abdullah looked at me carefully. "Manal, you are very dear to me and many others in the community. The Al Mitwakal family is powerful and rich. Whoever decided to mess with these girls has made a big mistake. Nobody in Baqubah believes it was these brothers, and all the police officers are saying there were never any ransom requests. My advice to you would be not to ask about these girls anymore. There are things you can do, and things you can't do. You need to become better at distinguishing between the two."

My heart sank at these words. I didn't need to look in Yusuf's direction to see the look on his face. He had already seen me stubbornly forge ahead with other risky cases, and I knew he was dreading that I was going to do it again.

* * *

A difficult situation had just become even more complicated. The girls' foolish behavior had not only put their lives at risk but had also resulted in the wrongful torture and imprisonment of two innocent brothers. Yusuf's sources confirmed Abdullah's statement that nobody believed the two brothers had kidnapped the girls.

They were from a poor family well known in their village for their piety. They were among a handful of villagers who spent every dawn praying in the local mosque. Somehow they had managed to become the perfect scapegoats.

Yusuf had done his homework about the Al Mitwakal family as well. They were a powerful tribal family that made its wealth from numerous chicken farms in several governorates south of Baghdad. They were well known in Baqubah as being among the handful of families who had managed to benefit from both the previous regime and the present situation. Their connections reached deep within the Iraqi police and local district councils. At the same time the Al Mitwakal family was also very close to the U.S. military base and had many contracts with the U.S. Army to support the reconstruction work. The family would not rest until they knew for sure what had happened to their girls. If not for love, then for honor. Abdullah's advice that this wasn't a family to be messed with was the understatement of the year.

All of Baqubah was up in arms about the girls' kidnapping, and the women's center that we worked with there was reporting an increase of young girls being pulled out of school for fear of kidnappings. My head hurt just thinking about the string of events that had been unleashed by these girls' actions.

Despite the chain of consequences, I still had sympathy for the girls. I had spent enough time in the central governorates surrounding Baghdad to know the difficulties girls like them faced. I knew many teenage girls who had been forced into marriage. The lucky ones managed to make their marriage work, but many of them would end up divorced and returned to their parents. Of course there were also the widows, the other pariahs in Iraqi society, right after the divorcees. The fact that these women were no longer virgins somehow meant that they were permanently in heat. Iraqi men labeled them as easy prey, and parents often kept their widowed or divorced daughters under lock and key. If a chastity belt had been marketed in Iraq, it would have become the nation's best-selling item.

Zeena and Rasha had approached the marriageable age, and I could easily imagine that they had panicked at the thought of falling into these circumstances. The fact that they were from a successful and powerful family would only seal their fate.

I had also spent enough time in people's homes to know how naive some girls were. Within Baghdad (with the exception of the ghettos), the girls were known as *Baghdadiyaat*. They were much more cosmopolitan and sophisticated; they enjoyed the same personal freedoms I had when I was growing up. The girls of the governorates—or *Muhafaazaat* (slang for an uncouth woman), as some *Baghdadiyaat* called them—led sheltered lives. With a few exceptions, girls living in the governorates were kept inside the home. If they weren't married, they were only permitted to leave the house for school or errands, and only with a male escort. Even the most liberal families forced the women in the household to keep themselves covered in public. In most cases, the head scarf was not enough. It was often expected that the woman would cover herself completely in a black abaya. Yet with the introduction of the Internet, satellite television, and mobile phones, the girls never needed to leave the house to be exposed to a whole new world.

For example, I once stayed with a family in Najaf, one of the most holy cities for Shias. It is home to the tomb of Imam Ali ibn Abi Talib, the nephew of the prophet Mohammed (peace be upon him) and the person whom Shias consider to be the first Islamic caliph. It is also the place where I was first introduced to *Star Academy*, an Arab-language version of *American Idol*. The family had six girls and a boy. The boy was considered the king of the castle, and to his credit, he played his role quite well. The girls spent the entire night watching *Star Academy* and stressing out as to who would be chosen to continue to the next level of the competition. During commercial breaks they would beg their mother to buy them posters of the latest Arabic pop idol, none of whom I recognized or cared to remember. They spent the rest of the night watching the Middle East Broadcast Channel (MBC), channel 2, which was playing back-to-back American action films.

This was the opposite extreme of what you could have seen on television before the U.S. invasion. Under Saddam, there were only official Iraqi channels. Schools commonly questioned young children about their favorite cartoons. Their answers were used as an indication of whether their parents had illegal access to satellite television, a crime punishable by death.

Given the shift from complete censorship to nonstop pop stars and car chases, I could understand how Zeena and the other girls could have had delusions of grandeur. In my heart I knew they were not to blame for the situation they had created. Still, they had managed to dig themselves into a pit and dragged the two innocent brothers from Baqubah with them.

* * *

I was glad I had confided in Yusuf. He proved to be indispensable in his support for helping me to work out the details of the case. Women for Women International focused on improving women's access to earning a livelihood in postconflict areas. There were few resources for dealing with cases involving violence, runaways, and the usual range of dramas that seemed to find their way to me. I could only get involved in such cases in a personal capacity. With everything that was going on inside Iraq, I wound up working around the clock. There were only a couple of Iraqi staff members, headed by Yusuf, who were willing to go the extra mile when it came to controversial cases.

After Abdullah briefed us, Yusuf took control of the logistics between the shelter in Sulaymaniyah and the colonel in the Green Zone. I was happy that things were progressing with the girls' case so I could follow up with Captain Murphy regarding to the two brothers in Baqubah.

When I told Anne Murphy what Abdullah had told us about the brothers, she refused to believe me.

"There's no way," she said. "I admit that we can be dumb, but we're not that dumb. We have the girls in our custody."

"Anne, trust me on this one," I said. "I wish I were wrong. You didn't see the look on my friend's face. Just make a few phone calls and check out the story for me."

She called me back in less than an hour. "Okay, I checked and double-checked. It seems like what you said may be true. There are two brothers being held, but the Iraqi and U.S. Military Police in Baqubah are not saying why. I'm all over this. If they really got false confessions out of them, I promise you I'm gonna raise hell."

I hung up and breathed a deep sigh of relief. With the combined efforts of Anne and Yusuf, it looked like we were going to make it through this mess.

* * *

By the end of the week Yusuf had confirmed the plans to move the girls to Sulaymaniyah. Just as I was getting ready to thank him for his spectacular work, I received a phone call from Captain Murphy. Her voice was a bit shaky, and I braced myself to hear that the brothers had died in prison. But she wasn't calling me about the brothers in Baqubah at all. Instead, she was calling to cancel the transport of the girls to the north.

"Don't take this personally," she said, "but the colonel wants you off the case."

"Why? What's happened?" I was shocked.

This wasn't the ending I had expected. We were so close to

having closure on the case. I was bewildered. One minute the colonel was begging me to take over their case, and the next he was pulling the plug?

Anne hesitated. "How well do you know the staff member that came for the intake interview?" she asked.

Without hesitation I responded that I knew her very well and had complete trust in the way she operates. Muna had more than proven her dedication and commitment for Women for Women International.

Anne said that the colonel believed she had threatened the girls, and now he wanted all NGOs off the case. It would be handled by the military.

"How?" I asked. The colonel had offered no solutions previously. What did he think he could do now?

She told me it was classified. I thanked her for the update and hung up the phone. I could not imagine what could have gone wrong. I had underestimated Zeena. Somehow, she had managed to get her way.

I called Muna and told her about the colonel's decision. She seemed as surprised by the news as I was. I asked her what happened in the last meeting and asked if she had said anything that could have been misinterpreted. Muna explained that she had followed the intake interview exactly as Khanim had outlined. The girls reiterated their desire to stay with the U.S. Army and emphasized that they would only go to the north as a last resort. Muna had grown frustrated with them and told them they were being insolent and ungrateful to those who were trying to help them.

I kept asking if she had lost her temper, but she insisted she had remained calm the entire time. Suddenly, all I could hear on the other end of the phone was breathing.

"Oh, no. Now I remember I said something that could be

twisted into a threat," Muna said. "They were so rude, I told them that if they were my daughters, I would have given them a *rashdee*— a slap."

Bingo.

That's all Zeena needed to get us out of the picture. She had won her battle. I wasn't so confident she would have the wits to win the war.

* * *

The next morning, Yusuf joined me on the office balcony for a cigarette. I wasn't a smoker, but I woke up that morning desperately wishing I were. I had asked my driver to stop by the cigarette kiosk on Haifa Street on the way to the Shawaka office. They sold single cigarettes, but I decided to buy a whole pack of Marlboro Lights. Now I was beating the pack against the back of my thumb. I wasn't sure why. I had seen professional smokers do it before opening a fresh pack, and I found it oddly soothing.

"So why are you so upset?" Yusuf asked. He took the pack from my hands, peeled off the plastic wrapper, opened the flip top, and handed me a cigarette. "You got what you wanted. You are off the case."

I stared at the flowing expanse of the Tigris River below. Our office's location along the river's edge made it one of my favorite places in Baghdad. I thought about what Yusuf said. In a way, he was right. I wanted off the case because I knew it could only end badly. On the other hand, I also knew there was no way of ensuring the younger girls' safety. And now I would never find out what happened to the wrongfully imprisoned brothers. I remember Abdullah's words about knowing when to intervene. I knew this was a fight I would have to sit out, but it didn't mean I had to be happy about it.

I trusted Abdullah enough to know better than to make further inquiries about the girls. Such questions would link me to their disappearance and start rumors.

I later learned that not only was I suspended from the case, but so was Captain Murphy for having recommended me. We were thereafter denied access to information about the case. To this day I have never been able to find out what happened to the runaway girls or the two young men accused of kidnapping them.

Chapter
Thirteen

LOCKED IN

I HAD ENVISIONED MY DEATH in Iraq many times.

It started off as my own anxiety manifesting itself into the form of worst-case scenarios. The scenarios usually centered on wrong-time and wrong-place deaths. I wasn't the only one. Over time this kind of thinking developed into a sadistic game between the expatriates as we all competed about the worst way to go.

As I stood straddling the toilet, yelling out the window for help, I could not help but realize I had a winner.

Thirty minutes earlier I had managed to lock myself inside the bathroom of one of our Baghdad women's centers, which we were renovating. Apparently the stalls were the last on the engineers list, as the door to my stall was jammed. The first ten minutes I had been paralyzed with horror as I realized that I had not only locked the stall but also locked the front door to the bathroom as well.

There was no logic to the fact that I had locked not one but two doors except that I was so exhausted that I was no longer thinking. And now I had to pay the price. After the initial shock wore off, I started to bang and yell on the stall, but to no avail. I then noticed that I still had a sliver of luck on my side, and the bathroom window was right above the stall in which I was locked. I climbed the toilet and started yelling.

Nothing.

It was almost sunset. The official opening of the women's centers was the next morning, and we had been working late hours to make sure the center would be ready in time. I shook my head as I realized that nobody could hear me. My imagination ran wild as I realized that it would be easy for the staff to think someone else had taken me home. I prepared myself to be alone for the next twenty-four hours in the Baghdad bathroom stall. A part of me was actually relieved at the thought of my staff thinking I was home and leaving me behind. It would be far less embarrassing than their figuring out their brilliant boss had locked herself in the bathroom.

Just as I accepted the idea that I had been left behind, I heard the outer door of the bathroom rattle. Then there was a knock. I started to yell.

"Manal?" It was Yusuf. He must have noticed I was missing. He must have combed the center room by room. I was so happy to hear his voice. I could actually feel tears welling in my eyes.

I anxiously waited in my stall as I heard pounding on the door. Yusuf must have been kicking in the door. Somewhere in the excitement I climbed back on the toilet, mentally cheering him on. Finally, the bathroom door swung open and Yusuf charged in. I could feel my face grow red as I imagined the sight that greeted him. There I was, my head peering over the bathroom stall, thrilled that I had been saved. Well, partially saved.

"What are you doing?" he asked.

I was tempted to give a snide response but realized I was not in the best position for it. "This door is locked too," I offered feebly.

Yusuf shook his head as he looked at the bathroom stall. By now Mais, Fadi, and other staff had arrived to witness the scene. I avoided Fadi's eyes, knowing that he would never let me forget this.

As it was impossible for Yusuf to kick in the door without the stall door bashing me, he went into the stall next to mine and climbed on the toilet.

"What are you doing?" It was my turn to ask him.

Yusuf did not respond. He waved me off my throne and started to climb over the bathroom stall. He plopped down in my stall and instructed me to squeeze myself against the back wall. He then kicked the door from the inside out. Everyone clapped as the stall swung open.

I smiled at him. I knew I should show some more gratitude, but I was embarrassed to the core. Here I was developing a center to empower women, and I was already playing a damsel in distress. With the worse setting possible.

That was the first hint that the eve of the women's center opening was headed for disaster. The next thing was a phone call from the U.S. Embassy. We had planned for the women's center to be opened on March 8, International Women's Day. It was also the day scheduled for the signing of the Transitional Administrative Law (TAL). There were a lot of debates over the TAL due to its weak language about protecting women's rights. Some genius in Ambassador Paul Bremer's office had recommended that he attend a women's center opening as a symbol of his dedication to Iraqi women. Our women's center opening.

My heart stopped the moment the press officer explained the plan. I closed my eyes, refusing to allow panic to sweep in. I calmly explained that the opening of the women's center was an event for Iraqi civil society, and we were not planning on having any U.S.

government officials present. I also explained that we had officially invited Iraq's human rights minister, Abdel Basset Turki, for the ribbon-cutting ceremony. A polite discussion followed, and a lot of talk about the importance of the U.S. government highlighting its short-term wins. I tried to remain insistent that the ambassador's presence would deflect from the main objective—the Iraqi women. I pointed out that his attendance at the opening would eclipse all other activities and speeches. It was not the introduction I wanted to present to the Iraqi women. The press officer very calmly responded with the words I had been dreading since the moment I had accepted the women's center project.

"It's our money," the press officer said.

During the first months of my time in Iraq I been cynical about cooperating with the military and dedicated myself to working directly within the communities. Yet the reality was that nonmilitary delivery was too slow.

I was having nightmares of all the girls I had been unable to help. Yusuf would remind me over and over of our successes, but the fact remained, we had not been able to make a direct difference. This was why the women's center project was so important to me. It was clear that women did not have any place of their own to go. I had traveled to Karbala and Hillah to see Fern Holland's work on the women's centers, and the impact was immediate. You could see the joy. The women's faces glowed with excitement as they floated between the computer and training rooms.

I wanted the same solid results. I was desperate for tangible change, so desperate that I became blind to the cost.

I spent the next four hours trying to negotiate that cost. I would not let the women's center be hijacked. It belonged to the Iraqi women, and the Iraqi minister of human rights was going to cut the damn ribbon. Nobody else. Even Capt. Anne Murphy stood on the opposite side, desperately trying to get me to understand that this was a good thing. The fact that Ambassador Bremer would attend the opening would garner attention from Washington's highest levels and could lead to broader support for women's issues. But I wasn't buying it. It was a Kodak moment that would jeopardize the future of our project.

In the end, we made a compromise I thought I could live with. Ambassador Bremer would not attend the official opening of the women's center. Instead, he would appear three hours prior to the official opening for an informal breakfast with some Iraqi women. I went one step further and insisted that we choose the women. He had already met with some elite women; it was time for him to meet some marginalized women from the areas of Baghdad he had never seen. Women from Shawaka, Sadr City, Shaalah, the neighborhoods I worked in every day.

The next day was a blur of activity. The morning breakfast with the ambassador went incredibly smoothly, with the main photo opportunity not being the women but the scene when the ambassador was forced to take off his infamous combat shoes to sit on the floor with the women. The Iraqi women asked him questions and primarily focused on the time line for the delivery of services. One woman from Shawaka grilled him on electricity. Another woman asked him what he was going to do to give widows access to their husband's pension. Paul Bremer smiled, drank tea, and avoided the direct questions with polite ambiguities. Nonetheless, it was deemed a success by all.

Just as the ambassador's land-and-air entourage disappeared, our other guests began to arrive. It went just as I had planned. There was no overlap between the invited Iraqi guests for the women's center and the ambassador's visit. The ribbon remained intact. Later in the day, we learned of a major victory for women's rights: the Iraqi Transitional Administrative Law—which included the goal of including 25 percent representation of women in the government—was signed. We hoped that the signing of this historic document on International Women's Day would not go unnoticed and would symbolize the role women would play in the future of Iraq.

The day ended with my sending out a silent prayer. I was thankful that it had been a smooth and joyous day. For a moment I actually believed I had averted a disastrous outcome.

* * *

By midmorning the following day my joy was destroyed in one fell swoop. As a team of my Iraqi staff traveled from Baghdad to Karbala on a training mission, two cars attacked a cargo truck in front of my staff's vehicle. It was pure serendipity that saved their lives. The attackers had driven past the team's car, and our driver had glanced over as the car passed. He noticed that all the passengers were wearing black and white checkered scarves wrapped around their faces like ski masks, with all but their eyes completely covered. Instinct kicked in, and he pressed on the brakes. Within seconds, the attackers shot at the cargo truck a few cars ahead of the trainers' vehicle. The truck jackknifed and created a roadblock.

Our driver's instinct to tap his brakes prevented him from slamming into the cars ahead. He quickly maneuvered a U-turn and sped away. The trainers later described their fear to me as they watched the attackers gun down each car that had slammed into another vehicle in the convoy, creating a highway slaughter.

Although the team had gained an extra few seconds to make a U-turn, their nightmare was far from over. A second car pulled out from the long line of cars and began to chase them. Gunshots were fired, and our driver expertly drove back via a familiar return route. This was the second instance where chance was on my team's side.

On an earlier trip to Karbala, our driver had been fighting off sleep. To keep himself awake, he had invented a game of counting potholes. After the ambush, his subconscious remembered each pothole, and he was able to swerve around them, gaining a needed advantage over the attackers.

In subsequent months, this roadway would be nicknamed the Triangle of Death. It was a road that Fern Holland traveled frequently. My first impulse as soon as I heard about the attack on the convoy was to send Fern an email: "Fern, my team was attacked on the road between Baghdad and Karbala. Please be careful! Call me when you get this."

Fern never read the email.

The next morning I heard the news that Fern had been brutally killed on the same road. She and her assistant, Salwa, were found dead in the trunk of an abandoned vehicle. It was speculated that they had been stopped at a false check point and assassinated. Later I learned that their bodies had been riddled with bullets.

Nothing could have prepared me for this shocking news. In the beginning I refused to believe it. I was convinced there was a misunderstanding. I could not believe that any Iraqi would want to harm Fern.

Even though all my contacts in Karbala confirmed the news, I still held on to an absurd hope that everyone was wrong. It wasn't until the captain of the local Iraqi police in Karbala called Yusuf that I began to accept reality. Then I collapsed.

Yusuf took me to my home in Hay Al Jammah. All I remember was that I cried myself to sleep. I learned firsthand how quickly an event could strike at one's very core and change one forever. In two days, I was transported from an emotional high of bliss and accomplishment to a low of complete terror and loss. The depth and feeling of loss were overwhelming: the loss of life, the loss of friends, and the unbelievable loss for Iraq. Although I stubbornly held on to the notion that our work needed to continue, blinded with a new sense of determination to ensure that Fern's and Salwa's deaths had not been in vain, from that moment my life in Iraq changed.

For weeks after Fern's brutal murder, I had recurring dreams of exchanges between the two of us. Sometimes my dreams focused on her threats to expose corruption in the CPA and among the contractors. I would caution her not to make too many enemies within the system. I would remind her we were still in a war zone and very much vulnerable to the external players surrounding us. But the most common dream centered around the days we had traveled together on site visits for the women's centers. I remembered with clarity our argument over the building in the Hillah city center. In my dreams I argued passionately with Fern about reasons to reject that building. I would beg her not to make enemies. The dreams never lasted to a final conclusion, but the message was clear. I should not have stayed silent.

FOUR MEN AND A LADY

I DECIDED TO STOP WEARING the traditional black clothes of mourning the day I moved into my new home in Baghdad's wealthier Mansour district. I had worn black since the day of Fern's and Salwa's funerals. I moved into my new home for similarly depressing reasons.

Their murders were considered a major turning point for civilians working inside Iraq: Fern was the first American female civilian working with the Coalition Provisional Authority to be killed in Iraq. Internationals and locals alike believed the fact that Fern and Salwa worked to help women was the reason they were targeted. There was a fear that the United States was attacking the social fabric of the community by empowering women.

Nobody in Iraq had expected me to wear the traditional black. I would like to say I did it out of respect for the local customs, but that would not be completely true. I did it because I needed to. I was experiencing an overwhelming level of sadness, and wearing black somehow allowed me to release it. It was a nod to those I had lost.

I later learned I was not alone. Many women in the areas where Fern and Salwa worked also wore black during the days of mourning after the loss of a loved one.

I did not wear the traditional abaya that was worn in the southern villages. I mixed and matched whatever black pants, shirts, and skirts I already had. Outfits I had bought with the intention of looking slimmer suddenly turned into my uniform of mourning. I never realized how much black clothing I actually owned, and I was surprised it could last me an entire month. Iraqi women wore black for a minimum of one year after the loss of a loved one. Many widows wore it for the rest of their lives.

I could not help but wonder who, if anyone, would wear black if I were to die?

During my time of mourning I was touched by the level of support I received from Yusuf's family. His mother, who had so kindly sent me pots of food, continued to send me home-cooked meals every other day, and she often insisted Yusuf bring me home to spend time with her. During these days, she would hold my hand and offer me words of comfort. I saw her as my mother in Iraq, and her sympathy helped in my healing process.

Hussein would often bring Maysoon, Yusuf's sister, to my house during these days as well. The days she was not able to come, she would call to make sure I was well.

It was the first week of April 2004, and the general situation was at its bleakest point since I had arrived nine months earlier. On the streets of Baghdad, over the course of one year, the description of the coalition had openly shifted from the army of liberation to the army of occupation. Only a few days before, four American civilians were ambushed and killed in the streets of Fallujah. The killings were followed by a public desecration of the victims' bodies. It was difficult for me to recognize the streets I had walked down only a few months ago as the same streets now being broadcast on Arabic satellite channels with the images of four mutilated and burned bodies.

The hospitality from the tribal families had made Fallujah one of my favorite places to visit. At the time it was a small, insignificant city in western Iraq. The only association I had with Fallujah was that it had the best kebabs in all of Iraq—a well-earned reputation agreed upon throughout the country. I knew there would be no more visits and no more kebabs. The image of the four bodies hanging from the bridge that I had driven under a few months ago would eclipse the renowned Iraqi dish and tribal hospitality for years to come.

American soldiers were now fighting a two-front war with the Sunni stronghold of Fallujah on one side and the Shia stronghold of Najaf on the other. The mosque across from my new house was calling for a national blood and food drive for the people of Fallujah and Najaf. There was a buzz of solidarity between the Shias and Sunnis in the streets of Baghdad as a protest march to Fallujah was planned in defiance of the U.S. coalition siege on the village. All the training organized by the coalition forces on networking and coalition building that had been directed toward the emerging civil society institutions seemed to have had an impact—on the wrong target group.

The tension that enveloped the country blurred the lines between friend and foe. My old neighborhood, Hay Al Jammah, had somehow made it to the top of the insurgents' list of hot spots. Waking up to windows shaking from a nearby roadside bomb had become a daily occurrence. The fact that I was a humanitarian aid worker certainly did not guarantee that I would not be targeted.

Before the Shawaka office was finished, my house and office were one and the same, and as a result many Iraqi organizations knew where I lived. The address was even registered with the Ministry of the Interior (MOI)—known within the expatriate community as the Ministry of Hate. International aid workers and journalists alike heard rumors of MOI torture chambers for Iraqis and kidnapped internationals.

Everything surrounding me showed the telltale signs of a new time for Iraq. Human Rights Minister Abdel Basset Turki—the man who had opened the Baghdad women's center—had resigned. He quit his post on April 8 in protest over the military offensives against Fallujah and Najaf. The building with a pool that I had been offered in the Karrada district, and which was subsequently occupied by the Kurdistan Democratic Party, was bombed. The women's center we had opened a month ago in Mustansiriya, across the bridge from Sadr City, now lay empty due to several attacks.

As things were deteriorating in Iraq, the Washington DC–based headquarters of Women for Women International made an executive decision that I was to leave my old house immediately and move to Mansour.

The house I moved into was at least four times the size of my home in Hay Al Jammah. It was at the end of a cul-de-sac and opened into a large garden that had been meticulously maintained. The garden was a short-term consolation. The new security procedures, which I received by email, highlighted that I should not sit in places that were visible. They also strictly forbade me from interacting with my neighbors. The name of the new game was low profile. Gone were the days of having breakfast with the family across the street or midafternoon tea in the garden of my landlord. During my first nine months in Iraq, I had been invited to two weddings, an engagement dinner, and a graduation. In my new neighborhood I was to do my best to go unnoticed.

From a security perspective it made sense. From a social perspective I was lonely. Each morning a different Iraqi employee from our office picked me up in a different car to take me to one of three office locations around Baghdad. By the end of the first week I could almost hear the theme song of *Mission: Impossible* playing in the background as my life began to resemble a bad Agent 007 pastiche. I had nothing to hide, and yet I traveled around Baghdad like a wanted woman.

* * *

One morning Fadi arrived an hour late. Although he worked as a logistics officer, he sometimes came instead of my usual driver, Salah. It was all part of the security procedures. Fadi's arrival didn't alarm me, because the security procedures recommended shifting time and routes regularly. It was when I got into the car and noticed the silence inside that I knew something was wrong. Fadi's car stereo was an extension of him. He always had to play the latest single from the Lebanese pop star Elissa. The volume of the radio was somehow connected to the gas pedal. As Fadi sped down the Baghdad highway, his music would be blasting, and when he approached traffic lights, he would automatically lower it. This fluctuation in volume would last for the entire journey. No music in Fadi's car was a sign of big trouble.

"What's happened now?" I asked.

He shook his head and told me he had overheard some bad news. I sighed. Fadi was renowned as a source of organizational gossip—and not just our organization. He had a wide network of connections with almost all the international organizations, including the UN. He often joked that hot-off-the-press information was an added advantage of regularly attending Sunday church services. Most of the news he passed on was legit. This morning, however, he only agreed to share his news after extracting a promise that I would forget what he was about to say.

Our headquarters was at it again, Fadi said. He had over-heard a conversation between the finance manager and the main office, and it appeared they were not convinced that moving homes was enough of a security precaution for me. They felt the situation inside Iraq did not look good. There was a clear standoff in Najaf, and the violence in Fallujah did not look like it would ease any time soon. They wanted to move me to Amman, Jordan.

I found the idea unbearable. Despite my promise to Fadi, I picked up the phone and called the main office to see if there was any truth to the rumor. I was reassured that such a decision would not happen unilaterally. Nonetheless, they said, they had concerns about keeping me—an American national—in the Red Zone.

The Red Zone? Since when were humanitarian organizations using that term? In 2003, the Red Zone had been part of the U.S. military terminology. It disturbed me that it was now being used by civilians. Another sign of the times.

Since when was my passport my only identity classification? Yes, I was an American, but my past year in the Iraqi community had to count for something. I knew there was a certain amount of protection I would receive as an Arab Muslim woman.

I launched into a monologue over the phone and passionately argued that nothing had changed and that the news and media outlets were dramatizing the situation. Our program had managed to enroll close to two thousand women, and several of them had opened microbusinesses. Were we ready to turn our back on them just as they were starting?

When they asked me about the status of other international humanitarian organizations, I grew silent. Almost all my colleagues from other humanitarian organizations had pulled out of Iraq over the last couple of months. The remaining few could be counted on two hands.

Yet, in my mind, it was irrelevant. I would not leave Iraq. I owed it to too many people to continue the program for women I'd started. I could not tolerate the idea of leaving midway through. The deaths of Fern and Salwa had made me even more resolute. I strongly believed that if I was creative and flexible, I could find a way to continue our programs. I just needed to shift gears. I needed a new beginning to adjust myself to the changing context inside Iraq.

The conversation ended with a clear assignment for me: I needed to provide a new solution that would expose me to less risk. I was not sure what the hell that meant, but I was happy that I was able to buy myself more time. I mumbled an apology to Fadi for breaking our deal and asked him to turn around and take me back home. I needed time to think. It was only when Fadi handed me a tissue that I became aware of the tears streaming down my cheeks.

* * *

Finding a solution should have been easier. I had argued with near hysteria that there were many different solutions to remaining inside Iraq and continuing our humanitarian work. Yet now, at the eleventh hour, I could not think of a single viable option. I refused to live inside the Green Zone. It made no sense to me. It would only seal me off from the rest of Iraq and alienate me from the very group for whom my programs were targeted—Iraqi women. As for living in the Red Zone, my only argument was if I was viewed as one of the good guys, the Iraqi community would protect me.

But I knew this assumption was pretty naive, not to mention arrogant. The lines between civilian and military had been blurred a long time ago. The distinction between a humanitarian aid worker, a journalist, a contractor, and a civilian officer in the military were opaque at best among the Iraqi population. Given that the first civilian casualties in Fallujah had turned out to be mercenaries employed by Blackwater Security Consulting, it was no wonder that Iraqis could not differentiate between civilians and soldiers. The Iraqi population was increasingly doubtful of the intentions of international aid workers inside Iraq, and the average Iraqi citizen could only think about how the tangible changes in their lives (electricity, water, food) had all either remained the same or become worse. Since many Iraqis had been convinced that the coalition forces would improve these things by leaps and bounds, their disappointment at the reality was great.

I could not think clearly and reverted to my main coping mechanism: cooking. In times of stress I usually resorted to any food that would allow me to do a lot of chopping. The first thing that popped into my mind was tabbouleh. I called Fadi for the list of ingredients: bulgur, mint, tomato, and spring onions. I got stuck when it came to parsley, the key ingredient. Fadi had no idea what parsley was. The Iraqi Arabic word for parsley was different than the one common among Arab speakers in the Levant. It was on the tip of my tongue, but I couldn't recall it. Desperate to lose myself at the chopping board, I told Fadi I would find out and call him back. I dialed Zeena, my Iraqi American friend in Washington DC who was on call for emergency moments like these to translate my Palestinian-American Arabic to Iraqi Arabic. *Krafas!* I slapped my palm against my forehead. I knew that was the word. Armed with the right word I started to dial Fadi's number.

Before I finished dialing the number I saw his car pull into the cul-de-sac. I was surprised he returned so quickly. Wasn't he going to wait on the parsley? Fadi was empty-handed but my disappointment was replaced with excitement at seeing Yusuf in the passenger seat. My entire staff had been extremely supportive in helping me to cope with Fern's loss, but none were as supportive as Yusuf. He had remained on call in the last few weeks, and he visited me almost every other day.

When I opened my front door, Fadi asked if they could come inside and talk. I nodded, bracing myself for more bad news.

"Would you like some tea?" I was behaving with uncharacteristic formality, but for some reason, I felt very nervous in front of them.

"Don't worry about tea," Fadi declared. "Yusuf and I have the perfect solution!" He energetically poured out their master plan. The two of them had decided that the only solution was for them to move in with me in the house in Mansour. Yusuf explained that all attempts to strengthen security could not eliminate the fact that I was a single non-Iraqi woman living alone, the easiest of targets.

As they saw it, the equation was simple: if I was willing to risk my life to work inside Iraq, then they were willing to risk their lives by staying by my side 24/7.

This time I was aware of my tears. I was so touched by this act of kindness that all I could do was put my head in my hands and sob. The feelings I had been unable to release over the past months all seemed to pour out of me at once. All inhibitions had disappeared, and I allowed myself to cry openly.

Not knowing what to do with a crying woman, Fadi and Yusuf gave me the space I needed. When my sobs gave way to silent tears, they came back into the kitchen. They resolutely insisted that there was no other solution.

Still, my first reaction was to refuse. No matter what they said, I knew this was beyond the call of duty. Even if I could ignore this fact, allowing them to move in would cross the line between employer and employee. It would put an end to an eight-hour work day and force them to work twenty-four-hour shifts.

In reality, that was only a quarter of my real fear. The main thing running through my mind was the question of what I would tell my mother. The news of my living with two men would be enough to give Mom a trans-Atlantic heart attack. In our culture, it's simply not done. There was a saying from the prophet Mohammed (peace be upon him) that when an unmarried man and woman are alone, they are accompanied by a third: Satan. Add two men and double that. I shook my head and explained how touched I was by the sentiment, but on many levels it was not an acceptable solution.

"Then you must leave," Yusuf exclaimed. "You cannot stay here alone. You will be killed or kidnapped before the summer. We will not be men if we stand by and let that happen. There are only two options: we move in or you move out."

I was stunned by his bluntness but begrudgingly realized he was right. This was probably the only solution. But I could not imagine the conversation I would have to have with my parents to explain the situation. Although I was almost thirty, I still needed their permission. And although I have been known to be a talented salesperson, this arrangement was going to be a tough sell.

I checked to make sure their families were aware of what they were thinking. I was truly touched by the conversation with Fadi's and Yusuf's mothers, who both reiterated the same sense of urgency in providing me protection. Convinced by Fadi and Yusuf's arguments, I agreed that I would discuss it further with my family and with headquarters.

Women for Women was happy with the arrangement, provided it was clear it was strictly voluntary and being done out of a personal rather than any professional commitment. My parents were not as easy to convince. The ideal solution in their mind was for me to get the hell out of Iraq. When he realized I would not accept this as an option, my father began to question me about the arrangements. I explained the layout of the house, describing it as a large villa with four bedrooms on the second level and a master bedroom on the ground floor. I would be taking the master bedroom that had an en suite bathroom. The boys would stay upstairs. The master bedroom had a lock, and I promised to lock it every night. Reluctantly, my father agreed it was better than my staying alone.

Up until then I had suppressed any feelings of hope. Once my father agreed, I openly celebrated. Finally, something was going my way. I decided that the cloud of misfortune over my head had blown away. After all, it was truly amazing that I was faced with absolutely no opposition. In any other context, the idea of a boss living with her staff—a Muslim woman living with male bachelors—would have been scandalous. Yet in the surreal backdrop of Baghdad, it seemed like the natural solution.

* * *

The next month was one of the worst in Iraq. Granted, over the next few years the contest for worst month would be hard to judge. But April 2004 is still one of the primary candidates. It was one of the first times the Shia cleric Muqtada al-Sadr was able to demonstrate the strength of his militia by confronting the coalition forces. The U.S. military responded robustly to the four Americans killed in Fallujah with a month-long siege that left hundreds of Iraqis dead and even more displaced, many of them women and children.

It was not a good month for U.S. soldiers either. In fact, it was the deadliest month for Americans since the 2003 invasion, with 135 soldiers killed. The road to the airport was now known as Death Row due to the large number of deaths from roadside bombings. By the end of April, fuel was added to the flames when news of the physical and sexual abuse of prisoners in the infamous Abu Ghraib Prison at the hands of U.S. troops hit the international news wires. The soldiers were the main ones to feel the impact of the news. Many needed to hold on to the belief that they were making the lives of Iraqis better, but the news of Abu Ghraib was demoralizing.

The news didn't have such a large impact on the Iraqis themselves, however. Throughout the previous year, most Iraqis knew very well what was happening inside the prison walls. For many Iraqis it just reinforced their belief in American double standards when it came to human rights and justice. Others were quick to point out it was nothing in comparison to the torture Saddam and his cronies subjected the people to.

The day after CBS aired Abu Ghraib photos on *60 Minutes*, I met with my friend Capt. Anne Murphy. I was shocked to see her in civilian clothes, a punishable offence subject to court-martial. She explained to me that she had voluntarily enlisted in the army because she believed it was her duty, but after seeing the photos of Abu Ghraib, she felt ashamed to wear her uniform.

* * *

During the worst incidents, I would be under house arrest, ordered so by my organization's security officer and headquarters. Sometimes I would not be able to leave the house for days. As much as I disliked it, I knew I was treading a thin line with my insistence on staying in Baghdad, and so I willingly acceded to all the additional security procedures.

Despite all that was going on outside, April was one of my best months on a personal level. Somehow the men in my house helped me to create my own protected bubble. On the days I was allowed outside, we established a routine that included all the necessary *Mission: Impossible*–like tactics needed to complete a workday. I still managed to visit the women's centers we had established in various districts across Baghdad, and I often met with Iraqi women's organizations with which I worked in close partnership. Meetings in the Green Zone were limited, though, because of rumors that insurgents were monitoring the checkpoints and that people were being followed.

I watched these events with dismay as they unfolded. How could I keep ignoring the fact that Baghdad was no longer safe when even seemingly harmless acts such as looking out a window could prove fatal?

The reality that I could easily be caught in a roadside bomb had slowly seeped into my conscious, and somewhere along the line I had come to terms with the concept of a wrong-time, wrong-place death. I made it a habit never to leave the house without completing my prayers and asking God for forgiveness.

* * *

Within twenty-four hours of Yusuf and Fadi's moving in, all awkwardness between my roommates and me disappeared. The house was large enough to accommodate us without infringing on my privacy. By the second night, Salah and Mais had joined us. It was a G-rated Iraqi version of MTV's *Real World*—only in a war zone.

In the evenings the guys and I stopped being work colleagues and became our own dysfunctional family of sorts. All the men except Salah were single, so most of them spent the entire day and night at my home. Soon the family expanded, and we developed our own extended community. Salah's wife and the kids would frequently drop by during the day, as did the mothers of the other men. They often brought pots of food, and we spent entire evenings gorging ourselves on home-cooked meals. The food quickly became legendary.

Every Friday morning Mais would go downtown to get us breakfast: *qahi wa qaymar*, a phyllo puff pastry with thick clotted cream. At lunchtime he would go to our office on the Tigris River and pick up fresh *masghouf* (an open cut river fish) to be grilled and spiced. But he wasn't just a delivery boy. Mais would often spend hours peeling an entire bag of potatoes and frying them for the best french fries I ever had.

I made desserts and was most renowned for my carrot cake, which was a new phenomenon for the men. Salah would usually coerce his wife into making something, and Fadi and Yusuf were responsible for the endless supply of Diet Cokes in the refrigerator. Who knew that those Fridays would become some of the best days of my life?

The only request the four men made was that I teach them English. I have never been a good teacher, so in the true American spirit I turned to my main learning tools: television and board games. I had the not-so-bright idea of starting with Scrabble. But when the vocabulary pool was limited to *dog, cat, run,* and *fun,* I realized we had to get more elementary. So we jumped into my DVD collection and started with *Finding Nemo.* It was no mean feat to get four Iraqi men to watch a cartoon, but I was never one for easy struggles. All movies included my constant commentary.

I created a syllabus of movies as my crash course to the American immigrant experience, starting with mafia flicks from *Carlito's Way* to *The Usual Suspects,* interspersed with *My Big Fat Greek Wedding, Selena,* and *American History X* to emphasize diversity.

When we did move back to games, such as Uno and Arabic Scrabble, they evolved into the ultimate battle of wits. As the only female among four Iraqi men, there was a lot of pressure to win. The symphony of gunshots was drowned out, and the bomb explosions that caused the windows to shake only added emphasis when I managed to take over another country in the game of world domination, Risk.

Soon, our lives centered on DVDs, board games, and food. I gained ten pounds during the first three weeks that the guys moved in. I wasn't the only one. The five of us started discussions for our internal competition to see who could lose the most weight. On the day that we decided to start our biggest loser competition, however, Mais brought home my favorite brownies from a bakery in Al Hamra, together with sour cream and onion Pringles, and dozens of different chocolate bars for our late-night moviethon. Mais explained this was our "farewell to food" party. We would eat all our favorite foods and start the diet the next day. I took one look at the junk food–laden coffee table and exclaimed, "Let's pig out!"

Four pairs of eyes stared at me with bewilderment. I tried to explain that pigging out meant eating to our hearts' content, but then I realized the pig allegory wasn't going to work. I had never thought of what an inappropriate phrase that was in a Muslim country where Islam forbids the eating of pigs. Mais quickly grasped the concept, however, and he was thrilled by the term. Thus our "Pig-Out Parties" were born.

Somehow the competition for who could lose the most weight was indefinitely postponed, and the farewell to food was extended from one final night to the weekend, to a week, to the resolution of the al-Sadr saga.

* * *

Although I was grateful to the men for staying at my home, I had to draw some lines. First was establishing a firm curfew. The citywide curfew that was sometimes imposed by the CPA was not enough of a deterrent. There were times when the guys wandered back to the house at midnight, even though we had agreed on a 10 p.m. curfew.

One night Mais did not return until 10:15. When he knocked at the door, I refused to open it unless he promised he would never be late again.

He agreed, and I let him in. Then he lugged a sack of potatoes into the kitchen and threw it on the table. Mais gave me a lopsided grin by way of apology. His grins had slowly come to symbolize my virtual security blanket. There was something about it that made me feel like everything was going to be all right.

Mais ripped the sack open and pulled out a potato. He held it up in the palm of his hand, saying, "I make the best fingers in Iraq."

I never figured out where that Iraqi euphemism came from, but that didn't make his french fries any less delicious.

"Nobody can know that I cook," Mais said. "It doesn't look very good for an Iraqi man to be behind the stove."

Mais loved to open his sentences with a conspiratorial whisper of "nobody can know." Two nights ago this statement followed one of his frequent visits to the Internet café: "Manal, nobody can know how much time I spend at the Internet café."

Mais was an emerging Arabian Don Juan, although he was embarrassed by the fact that his love connections were cyber-based. Most nights he would stay at the café until dawn and chat with girls online. He seemed to have skipped his adolescent years, and now that he was knocking at the door of thirty, he seemed hell-bent on getting as much Internet love as possible.

He would chat with two types of girls. He called them horizons and potentials. The horizons were girls from different countries who expanded his horizons. Potentials were Iraqi girls whom he would consider marrying. A true romantic, Mais spent most of his time chatting with potentials, often girls just a few blocks down the road.

"My lips are sealed," I promised.

His face was scrunched together as he concentrated on peeling the potatoes.

"Manal," he nonchalantly asked, "how do you know if you meet Mr. Right?"

I couldn't help but laugh. Mais was a six-foot-two, 250-pound, thirty-year-old man who always managed to come across as a love-struck adolescent.

Seeing as I didn't have much insight on the issue of love, I just shrugged my shoulders. "They say you know when you know," I offered unhelpfully. "Why don't you just meet a girl in a coffee shop?" I was not fully convinced of Mais's wooing activities on the Web.

Six months ago I would not have dared to ask such a question. As liberal as my family was on some issues, when it came to dating, the line was drawn at romantic relationships outside of marriage (a line drawn in most Muslim households). Yet I knew of many Iraqis who were dating or who had dated at one time or another. In fact, many of them were deeply intertwined in some love drama. As one Iraqi colleague put it, "In the midst of sanctions and war, our only pastime was falling in and out of love."

Mais shook his head. "I don't even want to think about what would happen if we were to get caught. I wouldn't even risk talking to her by phone. I am not that irresponsible. Anyway, it's over."

I said nothing.

A few minutes later Mais continued. "Her parents are Sunni, and they would never consider a Shia like me." He shrugged his shoulders, and I got the impression he was trying to pretend he didn't care.

He was remarkably efficient at his task of peeling the potatoes, and he was already a quarter of the way through the bag. He sliced the potatoes and slid them into the frying pan, stepping back as the hot oil spat at him.

"A year ago these sectarian differences wouldn't have been an issue," Mais said, commenting more to the pan than to me.

I knew he was right, but I could not think of anything helpful to say.

Lucky for me, I didn't have to think of anything to fill what was becoming an uncomfortable silence, because Yusuf burst into the kitchen.

"What the hell are you doing?" Yusuf asked Mais.

"Frying fingers," Mais answered.

"Its 11 p.m. Are you trying to kill us from a heart attack?"

Yusuf asked. Like me, our pig-out parties were taking a physical toll on Yusuf. He was slowly developing a potbelly, which he patted proudly. The rest of his body still remained remarkably lean, and I reluctantly admitted to myself how handsome Yusuf was.

My ideal man had always been tall and dark, a look that was a dime a dozen in Iraq. Yusuf was a noticeable exception, about my height and on the fair side. His dirty blond hair and hazel eyes made him a heartthrob to Iraqi women. He sported a marine haircut and had a preppie fashion sense that other men seemed to copy. Yusuf could easily pass for an American. In fact, on many occasions when we came to a checkpoint, soldiers would wave him through and stop me and ask for my ID.

It wasn't just his good looks that made him popular with the opposite sex. He had a certain charm about him. Although aware of his good looks, he still possessed a bashful charisma that made him endearing. I had seen his interaction with the female staff, and it was clear Yusuf was aware of his impact on women. For this reason, I had gone out of my way to emphasize my preference for darker men in front of him.

When he smiled at me in the kitchen, I realized I had been staring at him. I tried to refocus on Mais and prayed that I was not blushing.

Mais slid more peeled potatoes into the frying pan, which were now crackling loudly. Yusuf was not even waiting for an answer. He headed toward the refrigerator to pull out a bottle of Heinz catsup. He lifted it proudly with a grin and said, "The catsup that nearly cost me my life."

Yusuf had a special gift for exaggeration. He could retell the most mundane event with such spunk that it would become legendary within twenty-four hours. From the grin on his face I knew he was going to launch into his account of valiantly picking up the catsup for me from the Green Zone.

"Do you mind if we use your catsup? Seeing as I spent two hours at the security check point just to pick it up?" Yusuf asked.

"Yes, of course," I groaned.

"I mean, this has to be special catsup. Although I have to admit that if I knew at the time the reason I was putting my life in harm's way was to pick up a bottle of catsup, I would have definitely told you to jump off a bridge. At first I thought this was a code word for something else, that it was infused with hashish, but lo and behold—it really is only catsup." Yusuf turned to Mais and asked, "Did I tell you I spent two hours at the checkpoint?"

"Yes, you did. I think this is the one hundredth time," Fadi answered as he waltzed into the kitchen and started picking the cooked fries directly from the fry pan. Unlike Yusuf and me, nothing Fadi ate showed on him. And Lord knows he ate. Fadi could win a southern pie-eating contest any day. Yet he was all skin and bones.

"I am almost done with the first batch," Mais said and protectively swatted Fadi away.

"Just for the record, I did not know it was catsup either," I jumped in, feeling guilty. Anne Murphy had mentioned to Yusuf that she had a gift for me. He had volunteered to pick it up from the Green Zone the next time he was there. Aiming to please, he made a special visit just to pick up my gift. He was not too thrilled when he realized the gift was a bottle of catsup.

It was actually a very kind gift. The previous month I had mentioned how different Iraqi catsup tasted from the catsups back home. I had joked the one thing I missed was Heinz. Anne had thoughtfully remembered to ask for it to be included in one of her care packages. I was really touched she had remembered such a fleeting comment. It was just another indication of how thoughtful Captain Murphy was.

Mais placed a hot plate of steaming french fries on the kitchen table, and Yusuf squirted a generous amount of catsup over them. Within minutes the plate was empty.

"So what movie is it tonight?" asked Mais. Since Mais's English was the strongest, he enjoyed my movie collection the most. Yusuf and Fadi enjoyed the board games better.

In the end the exchange was pretty fair. They offered me around-the-clock protection and in return I introduced them to *The Godfather* movies and microwave popcorn.

* * *

Early the next morning Salah stopped by with his wife, Nagham, and his two children. I had spoken several times with Nagham on the phone, and sometimes she would drop by for a short visit. I groaned when I realized she had brought more food with her, although from the savory smell I knew we would be pigging out as soon as she left.

Salah introduced his two children—eight-year-old Ali and six-year-old Zahra. "See, even we Sunnis name our sons Ali," he teased, casting a look at Mais and Yusuf.

"Of course they do." Yusuf jumped in. "After all, it's the nephew of the Prophet, peace be upon him."

"Thanks so much for letting Salah come over so often. I really appreciate it," I interjected, turning toward Nagham to change the topic. The five of us had had this conversation about the differences and similarities between Sunnis and Shias in different shapes and sizes at least a thousand times over the past few weeks. I couldn't bear it if they were going to launch into that topic again.

"Please don't mention it," she replied. "You are our guest, and if our house was big enough, I would insist you stay with us. Anyway, Salah is not here nearly as often as he would like. He is very jealous that you are all bonding without him."

Speaking with Nagham was so pleasant that it came as a surprise when Salah slapped his thighs a few hours later, the Iraqi gesture that time has run out. He looked toward Nagham. "Are you planning on spending the night as well?"

We had been so engrossed in conversation that we hadn't real-ized a few hours had slipped by. It was the first time Salah's family had stayed so long. I really enjoyed the chance to get to know Nagham better. She had been so pleasant to speak with, and her children were so well behaved. The entire time we were talking, they had sat quietly watching television and allowed the two of us to engage each other. It was funny. I could not remember how our conversation had begun, but I had felt so comfortable with her that we were exchanging our life stories with each other. I shared with her my experiences of growing up in America, and she probed about life in America while wearing the *hijab*. She was curious about my personal struggles to be a practicing Muslim in a secular country.

Nagham also shared with me her love for school, and although she married Salah when she was only eighteen, she was still adamant about finding a way to continue her education. For now she was content to pour her love for school into her children, but she believed, when they were old enough, she would have a chance to go back to school. She felt lucky that Salah, unlike her brothers, was so open-minded and did not want more than two children. Her other siblings had a minimum of six children each.

Meanwhile, she shared with me her stories of the four men who were now my self-appointed bodyguards. I was always aware of the camaraderie between the four friends, but I never realized how deep their relationship was with one another.

Yusuf, Mais, and Fadi had been by Salah's side the first time Salah had come to ask for Nagham's hand in marriage. Nagham described how intimidated she was when she saw four young men coming through the door. The three of them had been by his side the day of his wedding. Each of the young men had come in their own car to make the most of the *zafah* (the wedding proces-sion), driving side by side with the wedding vehicle carrying the bride and groom, music blasting, horns honking, and occasionally shooting their revolvers into the sky. At the end of the wedding, the four friends shot their AK47s into the sky—the Iraqi version of firecrackers—to mark the wedding celebration.

Nagham told me the three of them were also standing with Salah in the waiting room when Ali was born. She described them as neighbors who became friends, friends who became brothers.

The whole time Nagham sat with me I could not help but stare in awe at her. I was stunned at how beautiful she was. Salah was a lot of things, but handsome was not one of them. In fact, he was far from it. But Nagham's tall, slim body concealed the fact that she was a mother of two. Her long black ebony hair hung down to her waist and stood in sharp contrast to her porcelain white skin. I was amazed at the length of her eyelashes, and I could have sworn I felt a small breeze every time she blinked. She had a Bedouin beauty about her that I had imagined when I read classical Arabic poetry. I could easily picture her as the muse of many of Iraq's poets.

After Salah and Nagham had driven off with their children, I stood staring out the front door for minutes. I was still struck by Nagham's beauty, or rather, more bluntly, at Salah's lack thereof. "How did that happen?" I asked Yusuf as I closed the door.

Yusuf laughed, knowing exactly what I meant. "She is his cousin," he said.

I laughed, pleased that the two of us understood each other so easily.

"This is listed among our unsolved mysteries, our Iraqi version of beauty and the beast," he added.

As Yusuf gently poked fun at his friend, I was struck once more with the compassion in his voice. I recalled Nagham's description of the way the four men had grown up together, sharing the most precious memories with one another.

Their friendship stood in defiance of talk of the inevitability of a segregated Iraq. As the situation inside Iraq disintegrated around me, I had the privilege of watching these four interact. They loved each other in a way Western culture reserved for blood brothers. Each one was quite literally prepared to take a bullet for the other.

And somehow I had been allowed into their circle.

* * *

Our bubble burst one afternoon when I received a call from Rayyan, the Iraqi manager of the Democracy and Transparency Institute (DTI), an American nonprofit organization. Part of my organization's new security guidelines was that if the situation were to deteriorate, I would be evacuated with the DTI team, and Rayyan had agreed to include me on all DTI security updates. By this point, though, I had read and ignored all his emails about the "Red Zone" and "emergency evacuation." I knew this was bad, but in my mind, although the situation had deteriorated, it was still controllable. Plus I had a Monopoly championship to hold on to.

Apparently, Rayyan and his team didn't believe the situation was safe anymore. He was calling from the Baghdad airport, where he had evacuated his team, chartered a plane, and planned to fly out in the next thirty minutes. He apologized profusely for not calling me sooner, but their security procedures stipulated that nobody was to be informed of evacuation plans until the last moment. Nobody. I didn't see the benefit of pointing out that we had a verbal agreement and that I was supposed to be a part of any evacuation plan. Dumbfounded, I just hung up the phone.

I told the news to the guys.

We had been in the middle of an intense game of Risk. The five of us were sitting around the living room table, playing the game by our own set of ad hoc rules. It was the third day of a headquarters-declared house arrest.

"Bastard! That selfish bastard!" Yusuf responded.

"What are you going to do?" Mais the pragmatist asked.

"Nothing," I said. "I am going to finish our game." I wanted to pretend like the phone call had never happened. I could not think of what could have prompted such a full evacuation. At the same time, I did not want to think about the fact that, given DTI's actions, the time for my evacuation had probably finally come.

"You have to go. They must have some information that you do not. We have to think of a way to get you to the airport."

Yusuf stood up and was pacing. Instead of being touched by his concern, I suddenly felt outraged at his sense of control.

"No, I don't have to go," I said. "I will stay. If it means a few weeks of house arrest, so be it. But I will not leave."

"Something has happened to make them decide to leave," Yusuf argued. "You are not only putting your life in danger, you are now putting all of our lives in danger. If I thought I could protect you, I would tell you to stay. But I know I can't. None of us can. So you have to go."

I could not begin to comprehend what he was saying. I started to shout, insisting that I would stay and that I could not leave. There was a part of me that recognized how immaturely I was behaving, but I could not stop myself. I felt a strong sense of self-loathing when I began to cry. Since when had I become an emotional fountain? I had never allowed myself to cry as much as I had these last few months. I saw it as a sign of weakness. At that moment I did not realize that Yusuf's words had hurt me. I had not realized that my insistence on staying was not simply an act of solidarity but largely selfish. The only word I was hearing from Yusuf was *go*, and it caused far more pain than I was ready to admit.

Fadi intervened before the argument could escalate. He pointed out that my leaving was a temporary solution. The fact that I was leaving now did not mean I was not coming back. It would do everyone some good if I were able to get out and have some time off.

I knew that everything they were saying was logical, but somewhere along the line I had forfeited my trust of logic.

Somewhere along the line Iraq had become an emotional issue for me. Personal.

The idea that I was putting my four protectors in danger finally caused me to relent. Reluctantly, I agreed to leave. The challenge now was how. Salah started calling to see if I could book a flight to Amman, since there was no time to get to the DTI flight. It turned out that all flights were over booked until the end of May. He was told it would be nearly impossible to get me on a plane.

Yusuf insisted I call the U.S. Embassy to see if there was a citizen evacuation plan. So I called. I received a respectful lecture on current travel restrictions on American citizens living inside Iraq. Once the employee finished reading the travel advisory, she told me that a bus transported people from the Green Zone to the airport. Then the embassy staffer explained that it would probably be safer for me to take a taxi. The bus was a prime target.

"It might as well be driving with a big fat red X on its roof," she said.

"Looks like we're on our own," Mais said after I told them this news.

Yusuf was pacing, repeatedly murmuring what a bastard Rayyan was for leaving me behind.

"I'm not his responsibility. When the shit hits the fan, everyone has to watch his own back," I said, wondering if that would apply to me one day.

"You don't believe that," Yusuf said. "More important, you would never do that," he added.

"Well, there's nothing we can do now," Fadi said. "So I suggest we get back to our game, and you all accept the fact that I'm about to kick your butt."

We all knew Fadi was right. The sun had set and there was nothing more we could do tonight. It was amazing how quickly we were able to fall back into our bubble. Over the next hour we were deeply immersed into the game. Mais was yelling at Fadi and Yusuf for forging an alliance, and Salah was taking advantage of the opportunity to slip a few extra cannons into the countries he occupied.

But news travels fast, and before the game was over I had received six phone calls: four from my mother, one from my younger brother, and one from our headquarters. Headquarters ordered me out of Iraq immediately. As to how, they weren't sure. They were irate with DTI's action, but they had no solutions to offer. Lest I forget, my mother wanted to repeatedly remind me how bad an idea my going to Iraq had been, and if I were to die, she would never forgive me. Meanwhile, my younger brother called to make sure I was aware I was killing our mother.

For the next twenty-four hours all five of us called every connection we had to book a seat for me on one of the outgoing planes. We then heard a rumor about the brutal beheading of a twentysomething American citizen, and by the end of the next day I was offering to sit on any plane's toilet seat if the airlines would just make an exception.

Finally, Lucie, a Lebanese friend who had strong connections with Royal Jordanian Airlines, negotiated a seat for me. I will always be indebted to her for getting me on that flight. Now the next task was finding a way to the airport.

The six miles between the Green Zone and the airport were probably the most dangerous strip of road in all of Baghdad. It was what the U.S. military called "target rich," and many international and Iraqi citizens were killed along that thoroughfare.

"We will take you," Yusuf said. His voice made it clear there was no room for negotiation. It didn't mean I wouldn't try. I insisted that I take a taxi because it would be less likely that anyone would attack an international in a local taxi. All four shook their heads. This was nonnegotiable. The next morning we would pack ourselves in a car and head for the airport road.

I broke the news to Maysoon later in the day. Although she agreed it was the best decision for me, she cried when I told her I was going to leave. I quickly added that I would be back, but I did not know when that would be or for how long I would be away.

I spent the early part of the evening praying in the corner of the dining room. Yusuf found me sitting there and reading verses from the Koran.

"It's nice to see you afraid," he said. " I was beginning to think you were a woman made of steel."

"I am not afraid," I said. "I just want to make sure that if something happens tomorrow, I'm prepared to meet my Lord." I did not mean for it to come out as cryptic as it sounded. I just needed to feel ready for whatever would face us in the morning. For some reason Yusuf found it funny and laughed. It was a kind laugh, and I was reminded of what a gentle person he was. A strong indescribable feeling tugged inside me, and I knew that, of all the people I was leaving behind, I would miss Yusuf the most.

"There is no cause for you to be dramatic yet. Things will calm down, and you will come back. You'd better—we have our birthday to celebrate." Our birthdays were only a day apart, and we had been joking about having a joint celebration. "You have three weeks to get yourself back here."

"Three weeks for what?" Mais walked in. Yusuf explained it would be our big birthday bash when I came back. Mais laughed and said there was no reason to wait for my return. We still had this evening. Despite having already passed the time for curfew, he planned to head out to Harthiya to get sandwiches from Time Out, the local hamburger joint. I shook my head with exasperation. Mais was willing to do anything for his stomach. I told him it was not worth it.

"There are some things worth risking your life for, and at the top of that list is a good sandwich," he said.

I have to admit, they were damn good sandwiches.

* * *

We would pig out until the very last minute. When I finished my morning prayer the next morning, I walked into the kitchen to see a fresh pot of tea and *qahi wa qaymar* on the table. I could not imagine how early they must have awakened to fetch my farewell breakfast.

When I got in the car a few hours later, I found all kinds of chocolate, sour cream and onion Pringles, a bag of Diet Cokes, and bottles of water. And the ride to the airport was only fifteen minutes from my house in Mansour!

The food wasn't enough to take the edge off. All of us were extremely nervous. Immediately we started debating as to which was the "least likely to get us killed" way to the airport.

The night before, we had run out to buy some Iraqi tapes—Fadi's way of ensuring I would not go into Iraq withdrawal while I was away. And so we ended the debate by blasting some music and just driving.

After ten minutes of constantly looking left and right like chickens, we realized that playing music on the thirty-ninth day of Muharram (the Shia holy time of mourning when all music and television is strictly forbidden) was not a good idea. As if perfectly timed, the moment we turned off the music, we turned a corner and saw a large cloud of smoke near the airport: the civilian bus had been attacked on its way to the airport.

The car was silent for about a minute (a record for us), and then the guys desperately tried to make me feel better by sharing the latest Iraqi jokes.

I realized how much I cared for them and felt really scared for how the day would end for them. I wasn't actually scared about getting blown up on the way to the airport. My worst fear was the guys' return journey home—without me. I could not live with myself if we made it to the airport, and then something happened to them on the way out.

I could hear the U.S. Embassy staffer's voice in my head, warning me that the civilian bus was a prime target. For the millionth time I realized how much I owed these guys for their selfless dedication to me.

As if God wanted to further remind me of the risks they were taking, up ahead two American tanks were responding to the attack on the bus. The tanks' gun barrels were moving, and somewhere between panic and instinct, the huge vehicles sped forward while their turrets simultaneously rotated. It was a frightening sight, with mere inches and seconds sparing the cars near the tanks. The large gun barrels swerved over them and knocked down lampposts on the roadside. The lampposts crashed down into the street. The only thing that spared our lives was Yusuf's driving skill.

When we got to the airport, I was told there was little or no chance of my getting on the plane. But somehow, armed with Lucie's magical connections, I was able to get my ticket. My boys stayed with me until I was ready to board. I was very sad to go, and despite the danger, I still wished I could stay. I felt guilty, being able to leave, having that choice to escape.

When I arrived in Amman, I heard that shortly after we had made it to the airport, the Baghdad airport had been closed.

My Royal Jordanian flight to Amman was the last one to leave for the next three weeks.

Chapter
Fifteen

BREAKING POINT

I REALIZED THAT I WAS slowly losing my mind the day I cornered a female Iraqi translator and began to grill her about her near-death experience. It was late May 2004, and I was back in Iraq after working from Amman for a few weeks. The situation was calmer, and I was even able to leave my house in Mansour to visit the women's centers. We now had three operational centers, although we had vacated our main office in Shawaka months ago due to the mini-battles that took place on Haifa Street. Despite the country's many setbacks, I was looking on the bright side, and I had hope that our programs would flourish again.

Our connections with the military still dogged us, to my annoyance, and every now and then a U.S. unit would stop in to check on one of the women's center. During one of the visits, a young Iraqi woman accompanied the soldiers as their translator. I had seen many translators before, but something struck me about this woman. She had an aura of strength, and I was impressed by her confidence. She also had a slight limp, and instinct told me this was something new. I found myself staring at her with curiosity.

She caught my eye and smiled. "You are either wondering about my limp, or you are thinking I am some sort of traitor for working with the Americans."

I was embarrassed at having been caught staring and openly confessed, "I am just thinking about how hard it is to be a female translator. I am an American, so I cannot say much to the traitor part."

She laughed and introduced herself as Raghad. She began by telling me how her team had been caught in a roadside bomb on the airport road. I was stunned. She described in detail the events of that horrible day: the sound of the explosion, the eruption of fire, and her realization that she might not make it out alive. She explained to me how, in the last few seconds before she passed out from the pain, her only thoughts were for her twelve-year-old son. Similarly, in the first few minutes after she woke up after a four-month coma, her only desire was to see her son.

"Why are you back at work?" I asked, shocked that after a near-death experience she would tempt fate so soon.

"The same reason I took the job in the first place," she answered. Raghad explained that she was a divorced mother, and her parents would not allow her to return to their home with her son. Raghad's husband had been abusive, and she could not bear the idea of leaving her son with him. When she was able to earn a substantial income, her parents had allowed her back in the home. In return, her earnings were given to her father at the end of the month. Raghad was happy with the arrangements, and she was pleased that her mother was looking after her son while she worked.

She shared her story with me with openness and sincerity. There was no motive behind her description of the events, and I was touched by her sweet, firm nature. What troubled me more than the gruesome details she shared was my need to hear more from her. I was disturbed at my desire to get a sense of how much pain was involved in her injury and recovery. It was only then that I realized I had begun to accept a brutal death as my fate.

This was a different form of acceptance than when I had first entered Iraq. Back then I had simply been aware of it. I had depended on my spirituality for support. I had tried to be more observant of my prayers five times a day, and I had even developed a list of people to whom I needed to apologize. In the last few months, though, my awareness had heightened. The memory of Fern Holland's death was still close to my heart. Whenever I left my house, I no longer simply say good-bye; I would ask people to forgive me for any misdeeds. At one point I even wrote a letter to my younger brother, Hani, with a deep sense of sorrow that I might not have a chance to know him better.

Yet these feelings were something different. While speaking with Raghad, death felt close. And I sensed an obsession within me to understand exactly what it entailed. Her answer, however, did not comfort me. Raghad described excruciating pain. I had always thought that the brain would protect itself and block the memory. But Raghad told me otherwise.

Three months later, Raghad's captain told me that she had been killed by a sniper. My only prayer was that her pain this time was minimal.

* * *

My obsession with death did not go away. Months slipped away, and I felt as if I were living in my own purgatory. Still, I refused to leave Iraq. There was no logic to it. I knew that I would not accomplish anything comparable to my achievements during my first six months in the country. Presently, Iraq was slipping into oblivion, yet the threat of pervasive danger had not reached the level it eventually would a few years later. I still held on to a fragment of hope that things would turn in the right direction. I still wanted to believe that all the work of the Iraqi women had not been in vain. My hope was rooted in the fact that the women's centers were operational again. Less than a month ago that would not have been possible. Yet we were still far from our destination, and I knew the road ahead was filled with many land mines.

I became more and more detached from the risks and occupational hazards. I mechanically followed our security procedures the day we found a small bomb outside the women's center in Mansour. I instructed the staff to evacuate the premises immediately while Salah, the only military-trained staff member, waited for the arrival of the army bomb squad. I indefinitely closed the women's center in Mustansiriya, across from Sadr City, when it was targeted by a drive-by shooting.

I obediently followed Yusuf's instructions and taped up my bedroom windows for fear of shrapnel. It quickly became second nature for me to hit the ground for cover the moment I heard a bomb go off. I took these actions like a robot, convinced they were a temporary necessity before the Iraqis were able to set right all that had gone wrong.

By the end of the summer of 2004, the situation in the streets of Baghdad had deteriorated as much as I ever could imagine. At that point, a hundred international aid workers, contractors, and journalists had been kidnapped, and twenty-three had been killed. And countless Iraqis had died. It only went to prove how limited my imagination was. A couple of years later, 2004 would be labeled as a stable time, with the years between 2005 and 2007 deemed as Iraq's dark ages. What I was witnessing was the onset of a major civil war; the nation was being torn apart in its infancy.

Part of my disillusionment came from the fact that Baghdad

was now lost to me. I could no longer walk the store-lined streets of Mansour, eat at the restaurants in Arassat Al-Hindya Street, or take a boat trip across the Tigris to shop for antiques on Mutanabi Street. Loitering in Iraqi restaurants was a distant memory. The only place I risked going was Yusuf's house, and even then only for a quick visit. I missed sitting on the Shawaka office's balcony overlooking the Tigris River. The mayor in Shawaka who used to nag Fadi about his parking was now dead, along with his two sons. My dear friend Reema Khalaf endured the trauma of negotiating her teenage son's ransom and had fled to Dubai the moment he was released. The neighbor across the street in my home in Hay Al Jammah who used to send me freshly baked pastries was now widowed. At every turn the Iraqi families I had become a part of were being ripped apart. It was arrogant to think that I would somehow be spared.

Yet deep down I continued to hope. During the summer of 2004 I was amazed by the stark difference between how a walk in the streets of Baghdad felt compared to only a year earlier. I was deeply depressed by how the situation had deteriorated, and I could not imagine it would get worse. Yet somehow, it always managed to do so.

During the weeks I was in Amman, Maysoon and Hussein visited me. It was the first time Maysoon had left Iraq, and the sight of progress around the small city of Amman made her realize how far behind her beloved Baghdad now lagged. I took the opportunity to play host and spent a lot of time with them. When Maysoon insisted on meeting my extended family in Jordan, I was happy to make the introductions. My parents were also arriving from the United States for a summer holiday, and I was eager to introduce them to the powerful Iraqi couple who had adopted me in Baghdad. Like many Iraqis, the more time Maysoon spent in Amman, the more she began to question the future of Iraq.

Then, in early September 2004, the kidnapping of two Italian aid workers made it clear that things could indeed get much worse. In this case, the difference was how the kidnapping unfolded. These aid workers weren't killed by a roadside bomb or seized at a fake police checkpoint. Their kidnapping was much more brazen.

In broad daylight, twenty armed men in business suits parked their GMC trucks outside the Italian NGO, marched in, and took the two women and their two Iraqi colleagues without firing a shot. Thereafter, stories of one of the Iraqi workers being dragged by her head scarf from the building filled my every thought. These kidnappings were the pinnacle of audacity, and it finally registered in my mind as an undisputable sign that anarchy reigned in Iraq.

I agreed to leave the country the moment Yusuf suggested it. I decided that we had reached another low point in Iraqi security, and I would again travel to Jordan for a few weeks. I accepted the departure with much more grace than my last send-off in April. Because these Iraqi families had virtually adopted me, I was among the only internationals still in the country. The diminishing traffic in and out of Iraq meant there was no difficulty in arranging for flights this time. Once again, Mais, Fadi, and Yusuf drove me to the airport. Once again, I left Baghdad with the full intention of returning shortly. I did not even notice that I was traveling on the third anniversary of the September 11 attacks.

* * *

And return I did. Three weeks after their kidnappings, the Italian aid workers were released. I was able to return to Baghdad, but only with elaborate security plans, even more enhanced than before. That did not deter me. I simply could not accept the reality that I was utterly useless in Iraq. Even when I heard about the kidnapping of Margaret Hassan, the director of the aid agency CARE, I was convinced it would be handled the same way as that of the Italian aid workers.

I was worried about Margaret, though. We had often found

ourselves on the same side during debates at the NGO Coordinating Council in Iraq, and I had a deep respect for her service in Iraq over the last three decades. Several local Iraqi organizations were holding vigils for her return. No other international kidnapping elicited the same amount of response from the local population. She had been taken in mid-October, and I was convinced she would be home by Halloween.

Looking back, my denial of any other outcome was a form of insanity. At this point, every American who worked or lived in Iraq had some form of professional security company that was responsible for their movements, or they never ventured outside of the Green Zone. My security operation was the same as the day I entered Iraq: Mais, Fadi, and Yusuf. I refused to organize long-term arrangements to live in the Green Zone. If that was my only option, it made more sense for me to live in Amman.

My breaking point manifested itself in the most selfish manner possible. It came during the holy month of Ramadan. This was my second Ramadan in Iraq, and although only a year had passed, it felt like a decade. I had plans to meet my parents for Eid—the celebration of the end of fasting—in Amman, and I was looking forward to the time off. A few days before Eid, however, the Iraqi government announced that the Baghdad airport would be closed indefinitely. The borders for people traveling by road would also be closed.

When I heard the news, I panicked. I had spent the last few months fighting to get in and stay in the country, and suddenly all I could think about was getting out.

Now!

With my dog.

There are moments when I feel ashamed of how I handled myself during those few days. I called Yusuf every hour, crying and begging him to find a way for me to get out of the country.

In between sobs I would ask him how I could take my dog, Ishta, with me. I had never before thought of taking Ishta with me to Jordan. However, something deep inside knew I would not be coming back to Iraq anytime soon. I could not bear the idea of leaving her behind.

I nearly went into hysterics when Yusuf told me that Ishta would most likely not be able to travel with me to Jordan. We still had not even determined if there was a way to get me out of the country, he tried to remind me.

For the first few days I refused to leave without Ishta. Yusuf had to enlist Zainab, the president of Women for Women International, to find a safe place for her. Zainab offered her uncle's farm in the southern governorate, a more secure area, as a new home. It was only weeks after I was safely in Jordan that I could remember with horror at how I extorted such a promise from Yusuf that he would personally deliver Ishta to the farm.

But my own problem was not as easily solved. There were absolutely no commercial flights out of the country. The only planes leaving Iraq were U.S. military flights to Kuwait City. Yet again I found myself forced to turn to Anne Murphy for help.

∗ ∗ ∗

The day I was evacuated, I was the only covered Muslim woman among a sea of military uniforms at Camp Victory, the U.S. military base adjacent to the Baghdad airport. Through my appearance, I became the de facto representative of the Iraqi people, fielding questions from almost every soldier I encountered. Why do they hate us? Why won't they let us help them? Why are they protecting al-Zarqawi (the chief al Qaeda leader in Iraq)?

By the time I arrived in Kuwait, I was emotionally drained and completely unprepared for the devastating news that greeted me the moment I landed: Margaret Hassan was believed to be dead.

For the next forty-eight hours I was inconsolable. I sobbed every second of the trip to Amman.

I desperately needed emotional support, but instead a Jordanian friend chastised me for crying over a foreigner while so many Iraqis were dying. The U.S. invasion of Iraq had polarized her thinking. Like so many others, her ability to empathize with human loss had been replaced with political zeal. Any iota of optimism I still had for the future faded.

Chapter
Sixteen

PURPLE THUMBS DON'T WASH OFF

THE SHOCK OF BEING FORCED to flee Iraq coupled with the news of Margaret Hassan's death forced me to acknowledge that Iraq's fragile stability had disintegrated and that my time there was probably over. Although my main interaction with Margaret had been through the NGO Coordinating Council in Iraq, I knew her story well. As an Irish citizen married to an Iraqi, she embodied the possibility of bridging the two worlds. She had lived in Iraq for three decades, and she had stayed in the country when even Iraqis had fled.

Despite this rude awakening, I was determined to stay in Jordan, which had become a crossroads for Iraqi intellectuals and international aid organizations, to continue my work to ensure a better future for Iraq's women.

I wanted a happy ending for my story. I didn't want to leave without it.

The fact that I had physically left Iraq did not mean I was ready to leave behind all the work we had done. Countless Iraqi women with whom I worked in Baghdad came to see me in Amman. Although the wear and tear of the "new" Iraq and the unbearable pain of their losses had aged them, they and their countrymen still possessed a stubborn determination to make things right.

At the same time, the number of my Iraqi friends now settling in Amman began to increase. Even more of them headed to Syria. We all waited for the end of 2004 with the belief that 2005 would bring some new promise.

During this time Yusuf and Fadi took a leave of absence from their work in Iraq and came to Amman for a two-month self-financed information technology and finance training course. Their presence eased my discomfort of working for Iraq from a distance. The three of us spearheaded an elections observation team for the out-of-the-country voting that would take place in January 2005.

Despite feelings of skepticism over their local leadership, Iraqis were proud of the fact that elections had been scheduled. The Iraqi women I spoke with promised this was going to be the turning point everyone had been waiting for. Yusuf and Fadi argued day and night about which political party would be elected. When a Jordanian commented that the elections were a farce, my friends' anger exploded. Despite almost two years of suffering, Iraqis took great pride in the democratic developments within their country. Yusuf passionately declared that other Arab countries were secretly jealous that Iraq was going to experience a truly democratic election.

"My Arab brothers just need to watch and learn. Iraqis are going to lead the way once more," Fadi teased.

Indeed, the new year would bring with it new hope for Iraq. The elections of January 2005 brought an astounding 70 percent of the population to the polls. After they cast their vote, Iraqis dipped their fingers in purple ink, and these ink-stained fingers became a badge of honor. Iraqis all over the world were giving a purple thumbs-up.

Iraqi women sent emails to me of their voting experiences. They described waking up early that morning, dressing in their best clothes, and heading to the polling stations. They described the patriotic fervor that infused the streets all across Iraq. Volunteers drove the elderly and disabled to the polling stations. Neighbors cooked for one another as if election day were a religious holiday. One woman wrote that she even took her children with her, despite the heightened security risk, to make sure they witnessed one of the proudest days in Iraqi history.

Fadi and Yusuf reported the same among the Iraqi expatriate community who had flooded the Jordanian schools to add their voices to their counterparts inside the country. Both Fadi and Yusuf came back waving their purple thumbs with pride. They described the long lines of Iraqis that had waited for hours to cast their vote. They sheepishly admitted to the number of fights they joined in when some Jordanians drove by and yelled crude remarks about Iraqis.

"Look," Fadi said as he aggressively scrubbed his thumb in the kitchen sink. "It does not come off! All the people saying there is fraud are liars." He pulled back his thumb and waved it at me, as if his thumb, which now resembled a raisin, was all the proof one needed to debunk the rumors of fraud.

The successful election was one reason to celebrate, but the news from Muna won me over. During a training session in Karbala, a discussion became centered on custody rights. The women began to share individual stories of losing custody of their young children to abusive husbands. Muna shared her own story. Afterward, one of the older participants came up to her.

"Your story sounds remarkably similar to the story of the mother of my son's fiancée," she said. "Where are you from?"

After a quick exchange, it became clear that Muna's story was indeed the same story; the woman's son was to marry Muna's long-estranged daughter. She arranged for Muna to meet her daughter after fourteen years of separation.

Muna called me in tears. "This is our reward for the work we have done. God has sent me my daughter!"

I feel foolish to have fallen for the hype of the new Iraq yet again. But being among the Iraqis at that time was once again euphoric.

* * *

Later I realized it was not only the election that had restored my hopes for Iraq. Being in Jordan, away from the war-torn environment that surrounded daily life in Iraq, I began to see Fadi and Yusuf in a different light. If they were not in training, they were by my side. It slowly dawned on me that this was beyond professional courtesy. We had developed very strong friendships, and our sense of mutual dedication went far beyond the workplace. Especially with regard to Yusuf.

During this time my body's protest over the last few months' trauma manifested itself physically. My back injury again flared up, and I needed a second surgery. Yusuf was by my side throughout the entire process, and his dedication and attention to me were unmistakable.

In Baghdad, I had practiced the Puritan work ethic of being obsessed with work during every waking hour. I had not thought much about my own social circumstances to the extent that I pushed the norms for an Arab American Muslim woman to the edges. I had given no thought to my personal life or my feelings. It was only in Jordan that I became aware of the feelings I had for Yusuf. It was more than simply being dependent on him in Baghdad. I realized how much I missed his presence. I realized that having him near me during a time of need had become second nature.

About a month after Fadi and Yusuf had arrived in Amman, Hussein appeared. He explained to me that Iraq was rapidly changing for the worse. Despite my hopes after the election, I was not surprised to hear this news.

The last time I had seen Hussein was at his parent's house in Khadamiyah. His father had been kidnapped and released, and it was customary to visit a family to congratulate them on the return home of one who had been kidnapped. I joined with Yusuf's family as they headed out to purchase a sheep to present to Hussein's family to celebrate Abu Hussein's safe return.

Given the situation, Hussein was hoping to move Maysoon and his children to Amman. For over a month I helped him look for an apartment and explore potential business ventures. After experiencing the grind of the Jordanian bureaucracy, however, Hussein's resolve began to falter.

Our roles reversed. I was now the host, the guide, and the insider when it came to the migration of Iraqis to Jordan. Hussein, Fadi, Yusuf, and I toured all of Jordan, exploring Amman in detail and checking out Madaba and the Dead Sea. There was bitter joy in these outings. It was great for them to see a new country, but every turn in the road only reminded them of their lost youth. At every opportunity, they would remark about how Iraq had slipped into the dark ages despite all its resources, while Jordan, a country lacking in natural resources had soared into the new millennium.

* * *

I would be lying if I said I was completely shocked when Yusuf finally declared his feelings for me. As I had acknowledged to myself, a part of me was aware of my feelings for him shortly after his first arrival in Amman. Still, I was taken by surprise when he actually said it. Yusuf explained his intention of getting to know me better outside of our work environment.

He picked the perfect location. A small group of Women for Women International headquarters staff and Iraqi staff were gathered for a strategic planning meeting at a Dead Sea resort in Jordan. The last few days of meetings had been surreal. Our mornings were spent brainstorming about where to take the activities of the organization, and our evenings were spent smoking shishas beside a magnificent pool. This was a completely different environment from that which we were accustomed to, and the feeling of normalcy was almost overwhelming. Those nights usually dragged past midnight and were filled with laughter as we recounted our various adventures in Iraq.

One evening we all decided to take a walk to view the Dead Sea during the still of the night. The hotel's cascading garden stretched about a mile from the pool to the edge of the Dead Sea. The garden was spectacular, filled with waterfalls, wooden bridges, and exotic flowers. Every five minutes someone from the group would stop to admire the scenery. By the time we reached the edge of the Dead Sea, it had been as if we had ventured through a wonderland. Everyone argued that the sight of the sea was anticlimactic and wanted to head back to the garden. I decided to linger a little longer, enjoying the complete bliss by staring at the historic sea. I loved the idea that I was standing at the very water's edge that prophets had walked. I was lost in thinking about nothing when I realized Yusuf had also stayed behind.

He and I turned to head back to the pool. The walk up to the hotel was more of a hike than the easy downward path. Yusuf paused near one of the waterfalls and sat down at the edge. He waved his hand in the air to get my attention.

"Hold up. Who exactly is chasing you? Can I at least catch my breath?" he asked all at once. Simultaneously he pulled out a pack of cigarettes.

"Come. Sit and enjoy the view," he said, patting the empty place next to him and offering me a cigarette.

"Not a really good way to catch your breath," I said as I sat next to him.

It was the first time I ever felt uneasy around Yusuf. My reaction, though, reflected his own obvious discomfort. He fidgeted with his cigarette and then began to share his feelings. He explained that he had romantic feelings for me and had been hesitant to approach me while we were in Baghdad. He recognized that my time in Iraq had placed me in a vulnerable position, and he had not wanted to further complicate my life. Yusuf confided that he also had not wanted to be seen as taking advantage of me during this susceptible time. Most important, he wanted to ensure our confidence in each other remained strong while in Iraq, and he had feared he would introduce an awkwardness between us. He confessed that for a long time he had contemplated asking for my hand in marriage, and he now wanted to explore that possibility with me.

I listened as he stumbled through his explanation. I knew that he was waiting for my own confessions, but I was not sure I was ready to share them. Deep inside I knew I had strong feelings for Yusuf, but I could not confidently admit where their roots were.

Was this really love? Or was it some version of the Stockholm syndrome? I had become so dependent on Yusuf for my survival and had placed my life in his hands in order to succeed at my work. There were always currents of adrenaline running between us as we tackled one problem after another. Was that the source of our emotions? Or was it truly something different? I had no way of knowing.

I shook off my feeling of unease and decided to disclose all my thoughts. The one thing Yusuf and I had always been able to do was speak openly and candidly to each other. I did not want that to stop now. I shared my concerns and fears, and he laughed as he admitted that he shared many of the same.

"That's why I want to approach your family. There is only one way to find out. We need to spend more time together, outside work. We have a great opportunity to do this while we are in Jordan, where we do not have the chaos of Iraq surrounding us."

As always, this pragmatic man who had become my solid rock was spot-on.

I could understand why he wanted to speak with my parents about an engagement. The concept of dating is alien to most Muslims, and the engagement phase is always seen as a preliminary official dating before the final step of marriage. Although I knew this was the normal approach for courtship, I felt rushed. I urged Yusuf to take his time before approaching my parents and to make sure he was confident of his feelings for me.

Yusuf once again laughed at me. I noticed his laugh now was different than the one I had heard in Iraq. This laugh seemed more intimate and private, and I sensed the nervousness underneath as he laid his heart open to me.

"Believe me," Yusuf said, "I have done all my research on this. Zainab says that it is very common for people who work in this field together to end up married. She knows many couples who have built very happy lives."

"You spoke to my boss about this?" I asked in shock.

"Well, she is my boss too," he said slowly. "Also, she is my friend. She is a wise woman, and before I opened the subject with you, I wanted to make sure this would have no impact on our work."

Yusuf went on to share Zainab's advice, and I sat there shaking my head. I was caught off guard that Yusuf had already put so much thought and planning into approaching me. I suddenly began to piece things together. How Yusuf insisted on introducing me to all his family. How Maysoon and Hussein had insisted on meeting my parents when they were in Amman. Even Fadi's questions during our long road trips became suspicious.

"So all this was planned?" I asked.

"Not really. None of it was planned. I would never intentionally chose to marry a Palestinian Sunni woman whose last name is Omar," he teased. (Omar is a highly contested figure in Shia political history.)

I laughed. When I first met Yusuf, he had strong anti-Palestinian feelings, and we would spend hours arguing about his discrimination toward Palestinians. During our trips to Najaf and Karbala, Yusuf would always introduce me as Manal Omarey, to avoid using my last name.

"Not to mention that I am older than you," I added.

He nodded. I could feel his eyes on me, imploring me to say more. All I could come up with was, "I cannot believe you spoke to my boss before you spoke to me."

Yusuf smiled. Yet again I noticed something new about his smile. He was a handsome man, and his soft brown eyes and round face gave him a teddy bear appearance. But his upper lip was crooked, which was further emphasized when he smiled. This gave Yusuf an almost gangster air, betraying the hardcore character hidden beneath the cuddly exterior.

"Well, Zainab is not the only person I spoke with. I also spoke with your aunts."

"What? When?" I asked.

Yusuf explained that during my time in the hospital for my back surgery, he had become very close to my cousins and aunts. Over time, he began to confide in them and explained that he intended to ask for my hand in marriage. He wanted to get a sense of my family's response before he approached my father.

"It was not planned," he quickly reassured me. "But your aunts are not fools. It was easy for them to figure out how much I cared for you."

"What did they say?" I asked.

Yusuf smiled triumphantly. "They said your family would be lucky to have me as a son-in-law."

I smiled. Yusuf's smile was contagious, and I felt a small tug deep inside. A part of me wanted to reassure him that indeed we would be lucky. He was a great man, and I could see him fitting in easily with my family. Yet there was a stronger feeling that this was happening too fast, and so I simply sat there and smiled at him. Fortunately, Yusuf always understood my cues and knew not to push further.

We sat in a comfortable silence for what seemed like forever, and without a word we made our way back to the hotel.

* * *

There was no doubt in my mind that our relationship had probably begun before Yusuf made this verbal commitment. The more I reviewed our past several months together, the more I recognized the unspoken intimacy that flourished between us.

Yusuf did not approach me directly after our conversation at the Dead Sea; Hussein became our primary intermediary. Once more, I realized it had not been a coincidence last summer that Maysoon and Hussein had insisted on meeting my family. Hussein was able to speak with confidence to the fact that, not only did Yusuf and I make a great match, but our families would merge perfectly together.

In the Islamic culture, dating is often frowned upon. The only proper way for a man and a woman to get to know each other is through an official engagement. Although I knew that to be true, I also knew my parents would want more of an assurance that I was committed to Yusuf than simply a desire to test the waters.

Hussein spent a lot of time pointing out the common ground between us, and he served as Yusuf's and my confidante as we decided the next step. Hussein pointed out that we had been fortunate to work side by side together, but without a proper engagement, we would never be able to take our relationship to the next level. Over time, I realized the wisdom of Hussein's words.

There was no doubt in my mind that I had feelings for Yusuf. The months in Jordan proved our feelings went beyond our work in Iraq. There was a personal connection. I knew that to truly discover the depths of my feelings I would need one-on-one time with Yusuf. I knew that could only happen if he were to approach my parents for permission.

The moment I gave a green light to Hussein for Yusuf's family to approach my parents, they shifted into gear. As I expected, my parents initially disapproved. They were so excited to have me out of Iraq, but they were not eager to have anything tie me to the war-torn country. Yusuf's persistence, however, succeeded, and eventually my parents were won over.

The more time Yusuf and I spent together in Amman, the clearer it became that we were right for each other. Within a short period of time I was able to admit what I had always known deep down: Yusuf and I were perfect together.

Chapter
Seventeen

IRAQI BRIDES

THE NEXT FEW WEEKS WERE pure bliss. Yusuf and I set a wedding date. He had returned to Iraq while I continued work through the Amman office. We planned to marry at the end of August in Amman. The situation in Iraq was still precarious, but we firmly held on to the belief that the summer after the elections would be a turning point for Iraq. Things would have to improve. We planned to get married, then I would return with him to Baghdad.

Perhaps it was the euphoria of love that blinded our vision. In reality, the situation in Iraq was continuing to deteriorate, and the violence was reaching deep into the homes of every Iraqi family. With the withdrawal of all international aid workers, the primary target of the insurgency became Iraqi civil society itself. Yet the stories seemed far away, and Yusuf and I continued to focus on the small signs of improvement.

Late one April night in Amman, I received the dreaded phone call all of my Iraqi friends got sooner or later. The news was shared with me very matter-of-factly: our dear friend Salah, who had also been one of my drivers, had vanished.

I couldn't believe that Salah had simply disappeared. This happened to other people, other organizations. We had taken every precaution and avoided all unnecessary risks. Yusuf was in Baghdad, and as soon as I heard the news, I called him to verify the information. The moment he answered the phone, I knew it was true. His voice was filled with sorrow and panic.

"I was just on the phone with him. He called me and said he was coming over," Yusuf repeated over and over.

We tried to recall the last moments we had heard from Salah. It became clear that his last phone call had been in the evening from an Internet café. Salah had called Yusuf to tell him he was coming over with some urgent news. Salah had insisted he could not give the details over the phone. Yusuf had waited for hours. He finally decided to call Nagham, Salah's wife. She had not heard anything from her husband since the morning. Yusuf instantly called the other team members and drove to the Internet café where Salah had last been seen. They confirmed he had been there. After that there was nothing.

For the next few days the search for Salah led to communiqués with everyone from the U.S. military and the infamous Ministry of the Interior to various militia groups. All the clues led to a dead end.

Over the next six months, we were sent on numerous wild-goose chases. At one point, the U.S. military confirmed that Salah had been picked up by the Ministry of the Interior. We demanded to see him. At the very least I wanted to provide Nagham with some verification that her husband was still alive. The more we pushed, the less information we received. Finally, both the U.S. military and the contacts we had in the Iraqi government came back with the same message: stop looking for Salah.

This was unacceptable. I continued to push, but by this time nobody would return my calls. A few weeks after Salah disappeared, armed gunmen came to Yusuf's parents home and asked for Yusuf. Fortunately, he was not home. The next day Yusuf's car windows were broken and his tires were slashed. A death threat was found on the driver's seat.

Fear and panic shot through all the staff at the organization. Salah's phone had been programmed with all their names and phone numbers. If he had been taken by a terrorist group, it was not unimaginable that they would try to extract the names of other Iraqi employees of a U.S.-based organization.

All of our offices were closed, and staff members began to work from home. Yusuf, Mais, and Fadi all left their parents' homes and stayed with extended family. They realized they would most likely be the next targets.

To this day, no trace of Salah, his car, or any of his belongings have been discovered. One of my thousand and one regrets of my time in Iraq is that I never called Nagham. I arranged for money to be sent through the staff to support her and her children while the search for Salah continued. But I could never personally call her; I did not know what to say. My reluctance initially started with a desire to call her only when I had good news to share. That day never came.

I used every connection I had in Iraq to pinpoint the smallest news on Salah. I begged Yusuf to continue the search. I believed that some news would emerge. If I could find any information of Salah, that was when I would call Nagham. But the weeks turned into months, and the months turned into years. There was no news of Salah.

The last time Yusuf visited Nagham was in the spring of 2007.

It had been two years since Salah's disappearance. Yusuf described how Nagham was packing all of Salah's winter clothes and taking out his spring wardrobe.

When he asked what she was doing, Nagham responded, "Everything must be in place when Salah returns."

It is hard to believe that there are thousands like Salah in Iraq. The trauma of their disappearance is only intensified by the family's lack of closure. Until there are revelations of the final, devastating truth, the lives of those left behind by the vanished are consumed with unrequited expectation and prayer.

* * *

My wedding day was the worst day of my life. I cannot remember any time that I had felt so fragile. The slightest incident easily pushed me over the edge. My heart was filled with a deep sense of horrible loss and sorrow.

The only day that could possibly compete with this awful day was the day our wedding was initially scheduled to take place, one week earlier.

The eve of our planned wedding day had been spent running errands and making the final preparations. My family had arrived from the United States weeks before, and Yusuf's family had flown in from Iraq. We had finally found a dabke (traditional dance) troop that specialized in popular Palestinian and Iraqi styles. My wedding dress had arrived from the United States, and my sister and I held a dress rehearsal to ensure there was no need for alterations. The dress fit perfectly.

We were planning to have the religious and civil ceremony in my parents' summer home, and the reception would follow three days later when the rest of Yusuf's extended family would arrive from Baghdad. Among the invitees still in Baghdad were his father and brother and Hussein, and they were scheduled to arrive the next morning. Yusuf and I were up late making the final arrangements when we received a phone call.

Hussein had been kidnapped.

That was the first bit of news we received. Yusuf and I immediately drove over to his family's apartment. Everyone was gathered around Maysoon and her children as she mechanically packed her things. She was returning by road to Baghdad at dawn. She wanted to ensure that no money or effort was spared during the ransom negotiations. And Maysoon was determined to be there when Hussein was released.

Yusuf began to pack his things too, planning to go with Maysoon. Hussein was his mentor, and he felt indebted to him for his years of support. In the last few weeks Hussein had been calling us every day with a countdown for the wedding, teasing Yusuf that he had a big surprise for our wedding day.

But Yusuf's family refused his plan to accompany his sister. The death threats that Yusuf had received were still fresh in everyone's mind.

During this time, the kidnappings of Iraqis had become an eerie norm. Just last year, we all keenly remembered, Hussein's father had been kidnapped and released. Several of Yusuf's, Mais's, and Fadi's extended families had experienced a similar fate. There was no reason to believe Hussein's kidnapping would be different. Foolishly, I promised Yusuf that everything would be fine. By the end of the week, Hussein would be sharing the traumatic events firsthand.

"Do you really believe we will ever see Hussein again?" Yusuf solemnly asked.

"*Ifaalo bel Khair, tajidoo* (Hope for good, and you will find it)," I said, quoting an Islamic proverb.

What I did not know at the time was that Hussein had already been brutally murdered. His family had misled us to believe he had been kidnapped because they did not want to panic Maysoon. They also feared that if the truth were known, Maysoon would not return. Under Iraqi law, upon Hussein's death, his children and his inheritance would revert to his family. If Maysoon were to stay in Jordan, Hussein's family would not be able to claim their grandchildren.

It was not until the next morning that Yusuf's family discovered the truth. Yusuf called me with the news.

The shock of Hussein's death was superseded by the reality that we had sent Maysoon and her children into Baghdad alone. Her mother, sister, aunts, and all the direct female relatives who traditionally would be by her side to comfort her were in Amman. I could think of nothing else except the moment when Maysoon would hear the news. I visualized her searching for us and finding no one.

The flowers that were delivered that day for the wedding were used for an impromptu mourning service in Amman. The food delivered was used to feed the guests who came to the house to offer their condolences and prayers. My perfect wedding dress remained hanging in my mother's closet in Jordan.

Yusuf's family desperately rushed to arrange transport back to Baghdad to attend the funeral with Maysoon. His mother begged Yusuf to stay behind. The word in Baghdad was that Hussein had known his killers, and it had been a well-orchestrated, targeted murder. Yusuf's neighborhood was filled with whispers about Yusuf's marriage to an American, and his mother pleaded for him not to return until it was safe.

My heart was torn. The selfish side of me wanted Yusuf to stay in Amman. The other side, the side that knew Yusuf, knew there was nothing more painful for him than being exiled from his homeland. The idea of Yusuf's being denied the opportunity to pay his respects to his beloved Hussein by attending his funeral was too abhorrent. Yusuf insisted on returning. I would not stand in his way.

In the end I did not have to. His mother's wailing made the final decision. She flung herself at his feet and swore she would not make it back to Baghdad alive if Yusuf would return. So Yusuf stayed.

The next morning Yusuf's entire family left Amman for Iraq. I sat across the room and watched Yusuf crouch by the empty stroller of Hussein's six-month-old son.

I could not bear the idea of Yusuf's being completely alone, but our moral beliefs did not allow me to be with him alone until after the official marriage ceremony. My cousin Tariq volunteered to stay with him until we made a decision about the wedding. To this day I feel a strong sense of debt mingled with envy toward Tariq for being by Yusuf's side at this time.

Every morning after dawn I would head out to meet them, and I would stay with Yusuf until after midnight, with my male cousin as our chaperone. Those hours of sleeping under a different roof might have just as well been decades. It felt unnatural to be far away. I desperately wanted to be by Yusuf's side.

As a result, we decided to get married at the end of the week, even though my parents wanted me to postpone the wedding indefinitely. They pointed out that we should wait for a time when we would feel like celebrating our union. But I could not bear the idea of a postponement. True, I had no desire to celebrate. At the same time, I could not bear the thought of being apart from Yusuf during this time. I wanted to be by his side 24/7. For two years Yusuf had been my rock. Now it was my turn.

The day of our wedding I sobbed from sunrise to sunset. A beautician patiently reapplied my makeup over and over. Although we had canceled the wedding reception, my parents insisted on having a dinner. Under Islamic customs, a wedding should be publicly announced. So my father invited a small number of our relatives in Jordan to a dinner to announce the wedding. To pretend to be happy in the midst of so much grief was torture for me.

It pained me that Yusuf was to be married without his family present. Every day his family called to make sure he would not return to Iraq. The word on the street was that he had married an American, and death threats were circulating as well. In the midst of her mourning, Maysoon called repeatedly, begging her brother not to return. She had lost her husband, she argued, and she could not bear the thought of losing her brother. Yusuf agreed to stay, but at great personal pain. He also reluctantly agreed to the dinner.

When Tariq and Yusuf came to pick me up from my parent's home, Yusuf was dressed in a suit with a smile plastered on his face. I rushed to the bathroom for my last flood of tears. I thought about all the days spent planning our wedding, the excitement, and our foolish persistence to be happy in the midst of all the chaos.

From the beginning of our planning for the wedding, his family had counseled us to avoid the evil eye and marry on the sly.

"Hide your love for one another! It is not a time for Iraqis to boast of anything good in their lives," his mother warned.

Yusuf and I had laughed at his mother's superstitiousness. We had made arrangements for our reception at the Intercontinental Hotel in Jordan and had invited our friends from across the globe. We deserved to be happy, we argued. But I could not shake off a strong feeling of guilt. If only we had listened, perhaps things would have turned out differently. Yusuf and I had stubbornly challenged fate. We had survived two years in the midst of war. We should have been grateful just to find each other. What had possessed us to flaunt it? My mind could not grasp the thought that Yusuf and I, with our optimism and perfect hope in our future, now had suffered a tragedy that had made our lives parallel to some of the women we had worked so hard to help.

I have trouble remembering the exact date of our wedding. I desperately want to block out the string of events that led to the tragedy of Hussein's death. In my head it all hinges on our wedding.

Our wedding is forever tied to his death.

Epilogue

DAWN APPROACHES

SEVEN YEARS LATER, YUSUF AND I remain on the sidelines with the sensation that we are not in control of our own destiny.

Given the number of death threats Yusuf received after our wedding, we decided to live in Jordan for the first year of our marriage.

Maysoon and her children moved out of their three-story villa in Baghdad and joined us in our three-bedroom apartment in Jordan. For years I longed to see Maysoon in one of her colorful scarves. Instead, she remained in the traditional black dress that marked her as a widow. Every day we called our family and friends in Iraq for the slightest indication that things were improving. But things were always getting worse. By 2006 the country was being ripped apart by civil war.

Everything I loved in Iraq was being destroyed. In 2007, a series of suicide bombs ripped across Mutanabi Street, shutting down the age-old book market for the next two years. The lives of the people I had grown to love were now being torn apart. Fadi's father passed away in the middle of the night. Due to the curfew, the family had to wait until morning to transport the body for burial. Hawzan, the eldest daughter of the Kurdish family that I lived with in Hay Al Jammah, suffered a cardiac arrest at the age of thirty-four after moving to Amman with the wave of refugees. Years later her father explained that she had died of a broken heart.

Despite the fact that I carried dual citizenship as a Jordanian American, there was no place for Yusuf and me in Amman. There, too, we constantly faced new obstacles. As an Iraqi, my husband was considered persona non grata. There was a window of time where Yusuf, like so many other proud Iraqis, was a man without a country, waiting in limbo for a new, valid Iraqi passport.

But we found a way to return to Iraq, this time in a different capacity. Our movements were limited, and the only safe space was within the Green Zone. We stayed there, but the zone by then was only half the area it had been originally.

Over the last few years I have worked to support local civil society groups, and Yusuf and I have helped with the preparation for the March 2010 elections. The civil war is waning, and Iraq has begun to emerge from the dark ages of 2007 and 2008. Iraqi friends and family discuss those years with glazed eyes, recalling the immense fear that overwhelmed every neighborhood.

Over the last few years, security and the surge of U.S. military efforts to hand over the country to the Iraqi government have overshadowed all attempts to make progress regarding women's issues. In fact, little work has been done to advance the status of women. The primary focus of everyone's efforts has been to stay alive. It is amazing to find ourselves having traveled full circle. The discussions on the ground are yet again on how to establish women's centers, and female victims of violence have no shelter other than a single women's center in the north. Today, the debate over Resolution 137 and its impact on the personal status laws for women has been revived, although the law has been renamed Article 41.

I have worked in other conflict-torn countries, but my time in Iraq haunts me more than any place I have been. I am unable to put the experience behind me. It maddens me that so many of the mistakes that pushed Iraq into chaos were avoidable. From the outset of the U.S. invasion, those in power in Iraq repeatedly betrayed the people of Iraq by standing on the sidelines as the society crumbled and by making promises that they could not keep. And I have a profound sense of guilt when I think of all the women whose cases I was never able to close. When I fled Iraq, I also fled from them, and I can't help but feel that I left them stranded. Iraqis are faced with a bleak dilemma: if they stay in their country, their lives are at risk, but if they leave the country, they are made to feel like a burden in their new homes. Essentially, they are forced to choose between death and humiliation.

Yet Iraqis continue to wait for the dawn.

Muna has carried forward the work of Women for Women International, pushing the program to help the most vulnerable women. She attended her daughter's wedding, and her son now lives with her in Najaf.

Mais married and moved to England, where he is continuing graduate school.

Fadi now lives in San Diego, where he is at the heart of the Iraqi social scene.

Maysoon and her three children resettled with Yusuf and me in northern Virginia.

Yusuf and I have dedicated our careers to Iraq.

Meanwhile, we watch the personal tragedies brought on by the growing insecurity within Iraq and the flight of Iraqis into neighboring countries while feelings of hope ebb. The chance that the international community will assist the Iraqis through their national crisis seems increasingly remote. The best hope for the Iraqi people is their own strength and conviction and their ability to take control of their own destiny. Having lived among them and seen their determination, I remain optimistic that they can make a better future for themselves. I can only pray that the international community and their own government don't stand in the way.

* * *

Over the past seven years, my most vivid dreams are about my experiences in Iraq. To my surprise, the person I dream about most is Fern Holland. Salah is second. My recurring dreams about him center around my begging Yusuf to continue to search for Salah.

I have only dreamed about Hussein once, but that dream is etched indelibly in my mind. It encapsulates all of my emotions toward Iraq.

In my dream, I experience Hussein in the same ways I experienced him in life: simple, gentle, and profound.

The dream starts with an awareness that there is a visitor in the other room, and I stand at the threshold of the door, knowing the visitor is Hussein. I do not want to go in, and I am surprised at the realization that I feel anger welling up inside me. For a second, I feel as if I am going to see a Hussein who has abandoned his wife and children to a cruel world, a man who has left them in a wilderness where dog eats dog, with no precautions or safeguards for their future. I do not want to see him. His energy calls out to me, and I think to myself, *He is here. I cannot disappoint him.*

I walk into the room and sit down across from him. We say nothing to each other. We do not have to, because the look on his face says it all. Do I really think this is what he wants? That at the ripe old age of thirty-two, he would have wanted to leave his family? For even a moment, do I believe this is easy on him?

I have never seen a face so full of expression. Regret and sorrow emanate from his entire being. Yet what rips at my heart is the look of longing in his eyes. He leans over to me and speaks of how beautiful Maysoon is. For a brief second he allows himself a wistful smile. I feel a twinge in my heart when I see the pride in his smile as he acknowledges his wife. The wistfulness passes, and his face becomes disfigured with pain. He tries to force a smile for me, but he fails. Instead, the sorrow in his face returns. A silence follows.

I can not find any words within me and have nothing to say. All I can think as the tears trickle down my face is that I am sorry. I have no right to be angry with him, and I am sorry that I blamed him. I think he hears me, because he nods.

He slaps his hands on his knees, just as he would do when he visited me in my house in Hay Al Jammah during what Yusuf and I refer to as the golden years. His gesture says, "Sitting here is great, but I must be moving on." Before he leaves he calls out to his three children. Fatima! Ali! Hamza! They come running into the room. I watch as they hug and kiss one another.

Hussein says, "Behave yourselves and be good to Manal."

They nod, and Fatima cheerily responds: "You do not need to remind us. We love her."

In my dream, Hussein and I exchange sincere smiles, albeit smiles of sadness and loss. He turns for one final glance at his children, and hope fills his eyes. Then he is gone.

READING GROUP GUIDE

1. As the author mentions in the beginning of the book, the title *Barefoot in Baghdad* refers to a popular Iraqi-Turkmen proverb that often serves as a warning to those who challenge societal norms. In what ways does Manal Omar challenge societal and cultural norms throughout her journey? What do you think it means to be a woman in chaos?

2. In Iraq, how people identify themselves across the spectrum of race, religion, and politics is central to their level of influence, acceptance, and safety in the war-torn environment. Omar carefully uses her unique, multidimensional identity to her advantage, utilizing her American citizenship, Palestinian heritage, and Muslim

upbringing to relate to a diverse group of people. In what ways does her multicultural identity serve as an advantage? Are there any times where you thought Omar's multicultural heritage may have served as a disadvantage to her?

3.   When the brutality in Iraq intensified, Omar writes that she had "begun to accept a brutal death as [her] fate" (205). Does this belief empower Omar by helping her conquer her fear of death? Or is she simply behaving recklessly, believing that she will die no matter what she does?

4.   Omar strongly believes that the advancement of women's rights is vital to the future of Iraq, even arguing that women's status in society "should be used as a barometer of success" (123). However, she notes that as an American woman working for a female-oriented organization, she is completely reliant on an all-male staff and the acceptance of the male community elders. Are laws like the "personal status laws" in Iraq an actual step toward rectifying the disparity in male and female rights, or do they merely perpetuate an illusion of fairness? Do you think true female equality is a realistic goal for the current generation of Iraqi women?

5.   Though she tries her hardest to maintain a rational perspective and focus on the individuals she is helping, Omar admits, "Somewhere along the line Iraq had become an emotional issue for me. Personal" (197). At what point in the memoir do you think Omar starts to become less objective and begins to approach the issues on an emotional and personal level? What effect does this have on her work in Iraq?

6. Due to the war and growing unrest, many Iraqi people are faced with the difficult decision to either stay in their country and risk their lives or leave their homes and become displaced refugees. "Essentially," Omar writes, "they are forced to choose between death and humiliation" (235). Faced with the same dire situation, would you stay and face death, or would you seek asylum in a foreign country, never to return to your homeland?

7. Though Omar and Yusuf are happily married and safe, Omar feels as though she has abandoned people, and she is haunted by the events in Iraq. Do you think Omar can remain optimistic about the future of Iraq?

8. During her time in Iraq, Omar comes across many women of different socioeconomic backgrounds, but stresses that she meets an astounding amount of "women engineers, lawyers, doctors—absolutely amazing Iraqi women who would put most American women to shame" (107). How do these women compare to the images of Iraqi women that appear in the media? Were you surprised to learn that there are a great deal of women who are not marginalized in society, have economic independence, and have a great deal of freedom in Iraq? How does this change your perception of Iraqi society and the situation for women there?

9. The motto of Women for Women International is "underpromise and overdeliver." Can you recall any specific examples where this motto can clearly be seen in Omar's work?

10. Fadi believes that music is something that can unite people across different cultures, and Omar finds a sense of normalcy and familiarity in cooking. What are other things that rise above cultural and personal differences to unify people and bring cross-cultural understanding?

11. Omar believes that "Charles Dickens understood war. 'It was the best of times, it was the worst of times.'" While the "worst of times" is a fairly obvious statement, what is meant by the "best of times" in a war-torn country? Are there positive things that occur in society or on a personal level even during an ongoing war?

ABOUT THE AUTHOR

3 Brothers Studio in Amman, Jordan

MANAL M. OMAR is the director of Iraq programs at the Center for Post-Conflict Peace and Stability Operations at the United States Institute of Peace (USIP). She served as USIP's chief of party in Baghdad from October 2009 to January 2010. Manal Omar joined USIP as a program officer for the grant program in August 2008. Previously, she was regional program manager for the Middle East for Oxfam–Great Britain, where she responded to humanitarian crises in Palestine and Lebanon. Omar has extensive experience in the Middle East.

She worked with Women for Women International as regional coordinator for Afghanistan, Iraq, and Sudan. Omar lived in Baghdad from 2003 to 2005 and set up operations in Iraq. She launched her career as a journalist in the Middle East in 1996. UNESCO recruited her to work on one of her first lead assignments in Iraq in 1997–1998. Omar worked more than three years with the World Bank's development economics group. She has carried out training programs on in Yemen, Bahrain, Afghanistan, Sudan, Lebanon, Occupied Palestinian Territories, Kenya, and many other countries.

Omar's activities have been profiled in the mainstream media by the *Washington Times*, the *L.A. Times*, the BBC, NPR, *Glamour*, the *London Times*, and *Newsweek*. Her articles and opinion pieces have appeared in the *Guardian*, the *Washington Post*, *Azizah* magazine (www.azizahmagazine.com), and *Islamica* magazine.

Omar is on the board of directors of Women Without Borders, an international NGO based in Austria, and she is an active member of the American Muslim community. She is also the founder and chairperson of the board for Asuda-USA, the sister organization for Asuda-Iraq, an organization dedicated to combating violence against women. In 2007 *Islamica* magazine named her one of the ten young visionaries shaping Islam in America. She holds an M.A. in Arab studies from Georgetown University and a B.A. in international relations from George Mason University.

Take action! You can help a woman survivor of war through Women for Women International.

As a sponsor, your pledge to contribute $27 per month to support one individual woman in our yearlong program of vocational and technical skills training, rights awareness, and leadership education will help a woman survivor of war rebuild her life, family, and community after the devastation of conflict. Your monthly contributions will also help your sister obtain basic necessities for her family, such as food, clean water, and medicine; pay school-related expenses for her children; or use the funds as seed capital to start an income-generating project. Perhaps more importantly, the letters you will exchange will provide an emotional lifeline to a woman who may have otherwise lost everything.

The sponsorship program links women from all over the world with women in Afghanistan, Bosnia and Herzegovina, the Democratic Republic of the Congo, Iraq, Kosovo, Nigeria, Rwanda, and Sudan who have survived war and violence. Individual sponsorships are a direct, personal, hands-on way for women in the United States and elsewhere to help marginalized women in postconflict countries. Help a woman survivor of war renew her hope for a better future today by visiting www.womenforwomen.org/sponsor-a-woman/sponsor-a-woman.php.